Income Tax Made Easy

TEACHER GUIDE

SECOND EDITION

PATRICIA PETHERBRIDGE-HERNANDEZ

AND

KATHLEEN P. O'DONNELL

J. WESTON

WALCH

PUBLISHER

Portland, Maine

We wish to acknowledge

the invaluable contributions of

Stephen O'Donnell, CPA, to this book.

1   2   3   4   5   6   7   8   9   10
ISBN 0-8251-3888-4
Copyright © 1994, 1999
J. Weston Walch, Publisher
P. O. Box 658 • Portland, Maine 04104-0658
Printed in the United States of America

Contents

Glossary   117

To the Teacher

Purpose

Although almost all workers must go through the annual rite of preparing tax return forms, most of us face it with trepidation.

We find it painful to part with our hard-earned money, difficult to deal with the forms, and just plain exasperating because we are never completely certain we haven't made mistakes or paid too much. Yet filing the tax return form is an integral and inevitable part of a worker's responsibilities.

In classrooms across the country, teachers prepare their students to become fully participating members of our society. Whether their focus is social studies, citizenship, economics, government, mathematics, parenting, or English as a second language, educators discuss income tax. We have aimed at making these materials a useful resource for teachers in all these fields.

Overview

We discuss a number of workplace issues: withholding, paychecks, deductions, and Social Security cards. Most importantly, we take readers step by step through the income tax process. We begin with an overview of taxes, gradually introduce essential concepts, and look at how our tax dollars are spent. We include vocabulary activities, puzzles, word searches, and questions to support the conceptual information. Finally, we discuss the forms and procedures for filling them out in a hands-on, simple, and informative manner. Case studies are provided for practice.

Our guiding principle has been to reduce the anxiety and intimidation people feel when confronting their income tax returns. Our materials include all the information students and teachers need for a course of study on federal income taxes. We believe that, taken a step at a time, the study of income taxes can be fun, comprehensible, and entertaining.

Background

This effort grew out of Patricia's first experience with income tax instruction nearly 20 years ago in a small rural community in northern California. She was asked to deliver a short two-day course for farmworkers on how to fill out 1040A forms, as a component of the English as a Second Language program. (The 1040EZ did not yet exist.) Initially, she took weekly groups of 10 and 20 people with their W-2 forms line by line through the 1040A form.

Although the local IRS was very supportive and provided wall charts and other materials, virtually no adequate classroom materials were available. Nevertheless, the response from the students was overwhelming. After they had completed their own forms, they went on to fill out the forms of their neighbors, aunts, uncles, cousins, and others. Patricia was interviewed a number of times on television, and the course became a regular program feature during the income tax season.

Positive Impact

The impact of doing your own income tax can be profound. Many people, especially immigrants, are wary of legal and civic obligations, and they often take their forms to be completed by

professionals. By going through the forms one line at a time and by applying some basic principles of cooperative education, students—whether adult or secondary—can develop a self-sufficient attitude. Also they may save themselves time and money. Quasi-legal responsibilities needn't be a mystery; with a little time and effort, they can be mastered. And what better place for this process to occur than in the classroom.

COURSE MATERIALS

Whether your goal is to discuss income tax in general terms or to teach your students to fill out the 1040EZ, the 1040A, or both, the course materials provide everything you need to know to direct a unit on income tax. Of course, it takes volumes to hold all the rules and fine points of federal income taxes, but this book presents the basic concepts that apply to most common situations.

Student Workbook

The student activity text discusses each concept in short, easy-to-handle topics. Chapters start with a list of topics and specialized vocabulary. (There is no vocabulary for Chapter 7.) A glossary defines the vocabulary words. Step-by-step instructions tell students how to complete the 1040EZ and 1040A forms. The 1040 (long form) is mentioned but not covered, because it is used to address more complex tax situations. Still, the basic concepts also apply to students who use this form. The Appendix provides information on and exercises for supplementary forms that many people must use in addition to the basic tax return forms.

Teacher Guide

The teacher guide contains all the information in the student activity text, plus answers on the activity pages, additional questions, extensions, and notes. The notes provide additional background information that you may find useful.

In addition, the first page of each chapter provides an overview, including topics, objectives, student activities, things you need, and important points to consider.

Since these materials can be used for many different types of classes and students, all the activities we suggest may not be appropriate for all situations. Disregard any activity that is not suitable for your students.

Important Notes

You should keep a few things in mind when using these materials. First, they are national in scope. They discuss federal income taxes. Because state and local taxes vary, you may wish to gather information on those taxes on your own.

Second, we used the latest information available to us when writing this book—for the 1998 tax year (filed by April 15, 1999). Each year, the amounts for deductions, exemptions, and the Tax Tables may change. Some rules may also change slightly. You should use the information in these

books as examples and emphasize to students that they should use current forms, and carefully review instructions, for their own tax returns.

FREE SUPPLEMENTARY MATERIALS

Though we may grudgingly send our money to the IRS at tax time, as educators we can be thankful that the IRS provides a wealth of materials that can be used in the classroom—most at no charge. For example, you may be able to get a wall chart of the 1040EZ and 1040A for the current year. Forms are readily available, as are informational pamphlets and booklets. We highly recommend that you obtain a copy of Publication 17 for your reference. Resources are discussed in Chapter 8 of this book.

It may also be possible for a speaker from the IRS or the VITA (Volunteer Income Tax Assistance) organization to visit your classroom. Since VITA volunteers help people fill out their tax return forms, you may organize a session with VITA to help your students complete their own forms.

ADDITIONAL MATERIALS RECOMMENDED

Although you can teach a course on income tax with no additional materials, you may wish to have the following items on hand. Many of them are available at no charge.

- Publication 17.

- Amounts of exemptions, deductions, and so on, for the current year.

- Extra 1040EZ and 1040A forms for the current year.

- W-4 forms (Withholding Allowance Certificate used by employers).

- SS-5 forms (application for Social Security card).

- Information about state and local taxes (look in your local phone book for the appropriate agencies).

- Telephone books, for exercise in Chapter 8.

- Ads and articles on income tax from newspapers and magazines.

- Books, videos, and other resources from the public library.

- Internet access

HINTS, TIPS, AND CAVEATS

- Make the classes as interactive as possible. Encourage students to ask questions. It can be easy to misunderstand some points.

- If students find explanations or instructions on the forms themselves to be frustrating and confusing, assure them that it is not their fault. The forms are often difficult to understand, even for professionals.

- Heed the disclaimer. These materials are not intended to provide tax advice but simply to explain basic concepts and provide practice in filling out forms.

- Try to customize your presentation for your students. Make sure they understand the utility of the information. Skip anything they do not need to know.

- Consider the interdisciplinary nature of the materials. You can address math, English (can students write better instructions?), history, and social studies (when did the federal income tax begin? what was its purpose?).

- When filling out the forms, go through each step slowly. The instructions may seem intimidating, but if carefully considered, they can be understood. Do not go on to the next step if the first step is unclear.

- Should you be presented with a unique or difficult tax question, the final chapter lists sources for assistance, much of it free. Refer students to these sources. Remind them that you are not a professional income tax preparer.

- You can use these course materials as a very short unit or as one that can be covered during a longer course, such as a semester.

- If you are comfortable with income taxes, you may create your own taxpayer scenarios and provide answer keys. If you use a computer with tax software, this is especially easy to do.

- Keep a copy of Publication 17 handy for reference. You may even wish to order enough for all your students. Publication 17 often highlights differences from the previous tax year.

- Because these materials reflect figures and rules for 1998, you may wish to familiarize yourself with any differences.

- Remind students that they should use current forms for their own tax returns.

- You could use this as an opportunity to help students complete their own tax forms. The best way to do this might be to arrange a special session with someone from the IRS or VITA, if available.

- If using students' personal information for exercises, be sensitive to their privacy. They may not wish to reveal their personal circumstances.

Final Note

The annual process of filing tax return forms is often discussed in the media with dread and anxiety. Although it is always a challenge to complete the forms properly, ignorance and the fear caused by ignorance can make the task appear to be all but impossible. Educators who work to explain the concepts and procedures to their students lead the way to a sense of mastery and self-sufficiency in an essential and inevitable aspect of their students' lives. Good luck, and have fun!

CHAPTER 1

Introduction

OVERVIEW

Topics

- Objectives
- Concepts
- Activities
- Benefits
- Disclaimer

Objectives

By the end of this chapter, the students will be able to:

- State the topics and objectives of the course.
- Identify benefits of completing the course.
- State that the course teaches basic concepts, is not comprehensive, and does not provide tax advice.

Student Activities

- Ask questions regarding course content.

Things You Need

- Course materials.

Important Points

- Ensure that students understand the purpose and intent of the course and the course materials.
- If you plan to include other activities, describe them during this chapter.

INTRODUCTION

Introduce the Course

If you earn money, you probably have to pay taxes on what you earn (your income). To figure out how much you must pay in taxes, you must fill out an income tax return every year. Filling out the form may not be easy, and parting with your hard-earned money may be painful. But doing this is your duty as a worker in the United States. It's part of being a member of our society. It's also the law.

Like many people, you may think it's too difficult and confusing to do your own tax return. That's not necessarily so. This course will take you step by step through the process, one form and one step at a time. You'll learn how to take care of this civic responsibility on your own.

Describe Chapter

This chapter introduces you to the course. In this chapter, we discuss the following items:

- **Objectives**

  You will learn what you will be able to do after you complete the course.

- **Concepts**

  We will discuss the topics and concepts included in the course.

- **Activities**

  We will describe the activities in the course.

- **Benefits**

  We will describe the benefits you will receive from completing the course.

- **Disclaimer**

  We will discuss what the course is *not* intended for.

OBJECTIVES

Identify objectives

After completing this course, you will be able to:

- Explain what the federal income tax is.
- Explain your filing responsibilities and deadlines.
- Fill out the simple forms most people use.
- Obtain more information about federal income taxes.

CONCEPTS

Identify course concepts

The concepts we will discuss include:

- What the income tax is.
- Withholding.
- Filing a tax return.
- Filing procedures.
- Types of forms.
- Filling out forms—1040EZ and 1040A.
- Where you can get help.

These are all concepts that every person who must pay taxes should know and understand.

ACTIVITIES

Describe activities

Describe the activities your students will complete during this course.

Activities in the course include:

- **Exercises with tax-related concepts.**

  There is a crossword puzzle, a true–false quiz, and a word search.

- **Exercises to help you practice using tax-related vocabulary.**

  Some words that you already know have a special meaning in tax situations, and you must understand the tax-related meaning. For example:

  file—"file a tax return," *claim*—"claim a dependent" or "claim an exemption." Other words may be new to you.

- **Exercises to help you understand how the concepts relate to your situation.**

  You need to understand this before you can fill out the forms.

- **Practice in filling out sample forms.**

  We will complete two different forms for people with different situations.

BENEFITS

Ask

Why is this information important to you?

- **You will have a better understanding of the process of paying taxes.**

- **Almost everyone who works must pay taxes and send in a tax return form.**

  This is your civic responsibility, and it is the law.

  You may need your tax return forms for immigration matters.

  You may get money back when you send in your tax return form.

- **You may be able to fill out the forms by yourself without paying someone else to do it.**

- **If you need help filling out the form, you will learn ways to get that help for free.**

Emphasize practicality

The concepts taught in this class are very practical and will help you in your life.

DISCLAIMER

NOTE: Make it clear to students what this course does not do.

Clarify purpose

It is important to understand the purpose of the course and your book, and what they are not.

- This book is intended to be an introduction to the basic concepts of income taxes and filing income tax returns.

- It is not intended to be used as professional tax advice.

- If you need more information, you should contact the IRS, an accountant, or a professional tax preparer.

- Rules and information change from year to year. Be sure to check the information and instructions for the current year.

Ask

Do you have any questions about what you will learn in this course?

NOTE: Describe how you will assign homework or outside activities. Discuss how you will grade students, if their work is to be graded.

If you plan to have a session where students work on their own tax returns in class, tell them about this now.

CHAPTER 2

What Is Income Tax?

OVERVIEW

Topics

- What kinds of income taxes there are
- What the federal income tax is used for
- How much the government spends
- Where the money goes
- How the money is distributed
- Benefits you receive
- What kind of income is taxed
- What kind of income is not taxed

Objectives

By the end of this chapter, the students will be able to:

- List types of income that can be taxed.
- Describe types of income tax.
- Describe tax-supported programs from which they benefit.

Student activities

- Match words and pictures.
- Practice using numbers.
- Identify types of income they earn.
- Identify kinds of government programs from which they benefit.

Things you need

- Information on your state's income tax.
- Information on any other income taxes for your state (for example, state disability insurance).

WHAT IS INCOME TAX?

Define income tax

Income tax is money you pay the government from the money you receive from work or interest.

Describe chapter

In this chapter, you will learn about:

- **What kinds of income taxes there are.**
  There is more than one kind of income tax.
- **What federal income tax is used for.**
  How the government spends your money.
- **How much the government spends.**
- **Where the money goes.**
  Tax money pays for many services, including Medicare, national defense, social programs, and law enforcement.
- **How the money is distributed.**
  The distribution of money can be seen visually on a pie chart.
- **Benefits you receive.**
  Benefits include education programs, federally funded highways, and medical research.
- **What kind of income is taxed.**
  Not all the money you receive is taxed.
- **What kind of income is not taxed.**
  Benefits from welfare, workers' compensation, and health insurance are not usually taxed.

Before we go any further, let's discuss the vocabulary for this chapter.

VOCABULARY

> **ACTIVITY:** Before providing the definitions, ask for volunteers to define each word. Write brief definitions on a transparency or on the blackboard.
>
> If you have more time, send volunteers to the board to record their definitions and have the class refine the sentence structure and spelling of each. You may also have the students use each word in a sentence.

Define vocabulary

Here are the definitions of the vocabulary words:

federal: Related to the government in Washington, D.C. Federal taxes are collected by the United States government.

state: Related to the government of the individual 50 U.S. states—for example, Oregon and Arkansas. State taxes are collected by the states.

income: Money you receive, such as your salary, tips, interest from the bank, and lottery winnings. These are only a few examples of income; there are many more types, such as alimony and money received from rentals.

tax: Money collected by either the state or the federal government to pay for the programs they support.

IRS: The Internal Revenue Service—the federal agency responsible for collecting tax moneys owed to the federal government.

earnings: Money you receive, usually from your employer.

> **ACTIVITY:** Have students circle the first instance of each word in the chapter.

WHAT KINDS OF TAXES ARE THERE?

> **ACTIVITY:** Begin discussion by asking students what kinds of taxes there are. List the taxes they mention on the board. Be sure that the ones in the student activity text are listed. Other types of taxes students may identify include sales tax, property tax, and local taxes.

Identify types of tax

There are several kinds of income taxes.

Federal income tax

- You pay a tax on your income to the United States (federal) government to pay for the cost of running the government and to pay for programs voted on by Congress.
- The IRS (Internal Revenue Service) is the government agency that is responsible for collecting income tax.

Social Security tax

- When you retire, or if you become disabled, you may receive Social Security checks.
- For this tax, you pay 6.2% of your income up to $72,600. Your employer also pays 6.2%.

Medicare

- This tax is used by the government to pay for Medicare, a medical insurance program for senior citizens.

- For this tax, you pay 1.45% on all of your income. Your employer also pays 1.45%. All wages are subject to the Medicare tax.

Mention FICA

Social Security and Medicare taxes used to be included in one type of tax called FICA. FICA stands for Federal Insurance Contributions Act.

NOTE: If you are self-employed, you pay both the worker's share of these taxes and the employer's share, that is, 12.4% (for income up to $72,600) for Social Security and 2.9% for Medicare on all of your income.

State income tax

- Most states require you to pay an income tax to the state. This is in addition to federal income tax.

NOTE: Tell students whether your state has an income tax.

Other

You may have to pay other kinds of income tax. This is different in each state.

- One example is SDI (State Disability Insurance) in California. This tax is used to help workers who are disabled in a way that prevents them from working.

NOTE: Discuss any other income taxes for your state.

WHAT IS FEDERAL INCOME TAX USED FOR?

ACTIVITY: Ask volunteers to define each word. You may also have them write their definitions on the board.

Describe uses of taxes

Your federal income taxes are used for many programs, for example:

1. **National defense** (Army, Navy, Air Force, Marines)—Pays for salaries, expenses, equipment.

2. **Transportation**—Money is given to state and local governments for highways, mass transit, and airports. Transportation money maintains the Coast Guard.

3. **Health**—Pays for Medicaid (health care for otherwise uninsured people), training and research, and consumer and worker safety. (Doesn't include Medicare and veterans' health programs.)

4. **Agriculture**—Provides money to help farmers. Pays for agricultural research. Prevents introduction of plant and animal pests and diseases.

5. **Education**—Money for elementary, secondary, and vocational education; aid to college students; training and employment services; research.

6. **International affairs**—Provides economic, military, and technical assistance to other nations. Pays for administration of foreign affairs and international organizations; maintains foreign exchange and information programs abroad.

7. **Science, energy, research**—Money for general science and basic research. Pays for space exploration and research to find ways to use space technology.

Other federal programs include natural resources and the environment, community and regional development, veterans' benefits, administration of justice, and general government.

NOTE: This information is often provided in IRS Publication 17, *Your Federal Income Tax*.

ACTIVITY: Ask the students how much money they think the U.S. government receives and how much they think it spends. Then ask them how much they think it spends on each of the programs just listed. Record their answers on the board. Then compare their answers with the information on the next few pages.

HOW MUCH DOES THE GOVERNMENT SPEND?

Explain figures

In the year 1997, the federal government:

- Received $1,579,000,000,000 (1 trillion 579 billion dollars; may also be written as $1.579 trillion)

- Spent $1,601,000,000,000 (1 trillion 601 billion dollars; may also be written as $1.601 trillion)

There was a deficit of $22,000,000,000 for that year. (22 billion)

Define deficit

Deficit means that more money was spent than was received.

Provide example

How big is one trillion dollars? Here's an example. It would take one million people earning one million dollars per year to get one trillion dollars. Or, it would take a person earning one million dollars per year a million years to earn one trillion dollars.

ACTIVITIES: Have students practice pronouncing each number out loud.

Review numbers, starting with very small numbers, and ending with billions and trillions.

Conduct a discussion of why there is a deficit and if the students think having a deficit is a good or a bad idea. Do students have a personal deficit? Do they ever run short?

NOTE: The government can't always predict the exact amount of taxes it will receive for a year because that depends on how much taxable income people (and corporations) earn. However, there has been a deficit for many years. The national debt is now in the trillions of dollars. A large percentage of federal income taxes is used to pay interest on the national debt. However, some economists believe that deficit spending can stimulate the economy.

WHERE DOES THE MONEY GO?

Describe expenditures

Here's how some of the money was spent:

• Social Security and Medicare	$ 608,380,000,000	38%
• National defense	$ 320,200,000,000	20%
• Interest payments	$ 240,150,000,000	15%
• Social programs	$ 192,120,000,000	12%
• Human and community development	$ 112,070,000,000	7%
• Health	$ 96,060,000,000	6%
• Law enforcement	$ 32,020,000,000	2%
Total	$1,601,000,000,000	100%

Remember that Social Security is not paid for by federal income tax, but by the Social Security income tax.

ACTIVITIES: If appropriate, have students practice pronouncing each number out loud.

You may wish to review the procedure for calculating percentages. (Divide the part by the whole; move decimal point two places to the right. For example, 608,380 ÷ 1,601,000M = 0.38, or 38%.)

If in the earlier activity you had students guess how much they thought the government spent for each type of program, compare their guesses with these figures.

You could also have students try to find out how much was spent in the last year and compare with 1997.

HOW IS THE MONEY DISTRIBUTED?

Describe chart (on page 6 of student activity text)

The chart shows the proportion of the total money spent.

This chart is called a pie chart because it is shaped like a pie. It is used to show how a whole (that is, federal expenditures) is divided into parts (that is, individual programs).

ACTIVITIES: Have students write the percentages from the previous page next to each item in the pie chart.

Ask the students what the largest and smallest items are. Remind them that Social Security is paid for by a separate tax.

Conduct a discussion or ask students to write about whether they think the proportions are appropriate. If they were our elected officials, would they allocate tax monies differently? How?

DO YOU RECEIVE BENEFITS?

ACTIVITY: Ask students if they receive benefits from federal government programs. Have them check the appropriate boxes. They may add their own items to the list.

Students should be able to state that they benefit in one of the following ways:

- Social Security payments when they retire.
- Access to education programs, Head Start, grants to schools.
- Medical research that finds treatments, cures, and ways of preventing illness.
- Using federally funded highways; having their food and consumer goods transported on highways.
- Safe skies through air traffic control.
- Veterans' benefits.
- Medicare benefits for senior citizens (Medicare).

WHAT KIND OF INCOME IS TAXED?

Define income

Income is earnings or money you receive.

- It is important to understand what the IRS considers income that can be taxed.
- Not all income is taxed.

Examples of income that can be taxed:

☐ Wages and salaries

☐ Tips

☐ Interest and dividends

☐ Rental income

☐ Gambling and lottery winnings

☐ Income from your own business

ACTIVITY: Ask volunteers to define each type of income listed. Have them write their definitions on the board.

Other income is taxed

Other kinds of income can be taxed.

Most people only have income from their jobs and from interest on a savings account. If you receive money from other sources, it is important to know if it is income that can be taxed.

ACTIVITY: Have students place a check next to the types of income they receive.

NOTE: Other kinds of income that can be taxed may include pensions and annuities, part of Social Security benefits (if received in addition to other income), alimony, royalties, bartering income, gain on the sale of personal items such as a car, and your share of estate and trust income.

If students are not sure if money they receive is taxable, they should check IRS publications or ask the IRS, an attorney, an accountant, or a tax preparer.

WHAT KIND OF INCOME IS NOT TAXED?

Identify nontaxable income

Examples of income that is usually not taxed include:

☐ Accident and health insurance benefits

☐ Welfare benefits

☐ Workers' compensation benefits

> **ACTIVITY:** Ask volunteers to define each type of income listed. If you have time, have them write their definitions on the board.

> **ACTIVITY:** Have students place a check next to the types of income they receive.

Identify other nontaxable income

Other kinds of income are not taxed.

NOTE: Other kinds of income that are generally not taxed include life insurance proceeds, meals and lodging provided by an employer, veterans' benefits, and part of scholarship and fellowship grants.

CHAPTER 3

What Is Withholding?

OVERVIEW

Topics

- Withholding
- Tax returns
- W-4 forms

Objectives

By the end of this chapter, the students will be able to:

- Explain withholding.
- Describe the purpose of the tax return.
- Complete a W-4 form for a simple situation.
- Answer questions about a sample pay stub.

Student activities

- Complete W-4 forms for two simple situations.
- Look at a pay stub and identify gross pay, how much of each kind of tax is withheld, and net pay.

Things you need

- We recommend that students bring their own pay stubs if they have them and use them in addition to the samples to complete the exercise.

WHAT IS WITHHOLDING?

Describe chapter

In this chapter, you will learn about:

- **Withholding**

  This is money your employer deducts (or subtracts) from your pay.

- **Tax returns**

  A form almost everyone with an income must file every year.

- **W-4 forms**

  A form you fill out for your employer to tell how much your withholding should be.

Before we go any further, let's discuss the vocabulary for this chapter.

VOCABULARY

> **ACTIVITY:** Before providing the definitions, ask for volunteers to define each word. Write brief definitions on a transparency or on the blackboard, or send volunteers to the board to record their definitions, and have the class refine the sentence structure and spelling for each.

Have the students use each word in a sentence.

employer: The person or company that hires you to work.

withhold: To deduct money from your pay. Your employer withholds money from your paycheck to pay federal and state taxes.

gross pay: Total amount of pay you earn before your employer withholds federal and state taxes.

net pay: Amount of pay you receive after your employer withholds federal and state taxes.

tax return: Report you file every year to calculate your exact tax bill. Examples of tax return forms are the 1040EZ and 1040A.

W-4 form: Form completed by the employee that tells the employer the amount of money that should be deducted from the gross pay and sent to the federal and state government as taxes.

> **ACTIVITY:** Have students circle the first instance of each word in the chapter.

WITHHOLDING

Ask

Have you noticed that there is a big difference between the amount of your salary, or gross pay, and your take-home, or net, pay?

The difference is because of withholding.

Describe withholding

If you are employed, the law requires your employer to withhold a part of your income to pay your taxes. This means that your employer takes out a portion of your salary.

- **The employer sends this money to the government.**
- **The amount of money the employer withholds is an estimate of your total tax bill.**

    People with the same income may owe different amounts of taxes because their situations are different.

Discuss example

Even if everyone in the room earned $500 a week, some people would receive different amounts of take-home pay. If Ramon is single with no children, he may take home $375. If Latisha is single and has two children, she may take home $425. If Sebastian is married and has

six children, but his wife doesn't work, he may take home $460.

NOTE: Money may be withheld for federal income tax, state income tax, Social Security and Medicare, and other taxes such as state disability insurance.

Other money may be deducted from paychecks, such as union dues, pension contributions, and health insurance payments.

TAX RETURN

Discuss too much/little withheld

Since everybody's situation is different, too much or too little money may be withheld from your salary to pay your tax bill.

- The tax return form is used to calculate your tax bill.
- If too much tax is withheld, you receive a refund when you file your tax return form.
- If not enough tax is withheld, you must pay more taxes when you file your tax return form.

You will learn how to complete the tax return in later chapters.

W-4 FORM

Describe W-4 form

You tell the employer how much to withhold by filling out a W-4 form. You can fill out a new W-4 form at any time. Usually, you fill out a W-4 form in the following situations:

- You start a new job.
- You get married or divorced.

- You have a child.
- Your child moves out and no longer receives your financial support.

This form tells your employer how much tax to withhold from your salary. You need a W-4 form for each employer. If you have two jobs, you must fill out a W-4 form for each employer.

Ask

If you have a job, you have probably filled out a form like the one in your student activity text. Does anyone remember filling out this form?

Refer to W-4 form

Look at the form. The W-4 form itself is on the bottom part of the Form W-4 page. You fill this out once you have calculated the amount you want withheld.

Mention worksheets

On the Personal Allowances Worksheet portion of the form, you write down the number of allowances you can claim.

- The more allowances you have, the less tax is withheld.
- You get one allowance each for yourself, your spouse, and your dependents (usually children).
- You do not have to take any allowances, or you can take fewer allowances than you are entitled to.
- You can also have extra money withheld from your paycheck to make sure you won't have to pay extra taxes when you file your tax return.

NOTE: The W-4 form is mentioned here briefly so that students know how their taxes are withheld. If students are employed, they have already filled out this form. We suggest that you keep this discussion general, since the W-4 form has terms and concepts that are discussed later in this course. In addition, the focus of the course is on filing the tax return form, not the W-4.

W-4 FORM—PAGE 1

Form W-4 (1999)

Purpose. Complete Form W-4 so your employer can withhold the correct Federal income tax from your pay. Because your tax situation may change, you may want to refigure your withholding each year.

Exemption from withholding. If you are exempt, complete only lines 1, 2, 3, 4, and 7, and sign the form to validate it. Your exemption for 1999 expires February 16, 2000.

Note: *You cannot claim exemption from withholding if (1) your income exceeds $700 and includes more than $250 of unearned income (e.g., interest and dividends) and (2) another person can claim you as a dependent on their tax return.*

Basic instructions. If you are not exempt, complete the Personal Allowances Worksheet. The worksheets on page 2 adjust your withholding allowances based on itemized deductions, adjustments to income, or two-earner/two-job situations. Complete all worksheets that apply. They will help you figure the number of withholding allowances you are entitled to claim. **However, you may claim fewer allowances.**

Child tax and higher education credits. For details on adjusting withholding for these and other credits, see **Pub. 919,** Is My Withholding Correct for 1999?

Head of household. Generally, you may claim head of household filing status on your tax return only if you are unmarried and pay more than 50% of the costs of keeping up a home for yourself and your dependent(s) or other qualifying individuals. See line **E** below.

Nonwage income. If you have a large amount of nonwage income, such as interest or dividends, you should consider making estimated tax payments using Form 1040-ES. Otherwise, you may owe additional tax.

Two earners/two jobs. If you have a working spouse or more than one job, figure the total number of allowances you are entitled to claim on all jobs using worksheets from only one Form W-4. Your withholding will usually be most accurate when all allowances are claimed on the Form W-4 prepared for the highest paying job and zero allowances are claimed for the others.

Check your withholding. After your Form W-4 takes effect, use Pub. 919 to see how the dollar amount you are having withheld compares to your estimated total annual tax. Get Pub. 919 especially if you used the Two-Earner/Two-Job Worksheet and your earnings exceed $150,000 (Single) or $200,000 (Married).

Recent name change? If your name on line 1 differs from that shown on your social security card, call 1-800-772-1213 for a new social security card.

Personal Allowances Worksheet

A   Enter "1" for **yourself** if no one else can claim you as a dependent . . . .   **A** _____

B   Enter "1" if:
- You are single and have only one job; or
- You are married, have only one job, and your spouse does not work; or
- Your wages from a second job or your spouse's wages (or the total of both) are $1,000 or less.   **B** _____

C   Enter "1" for your **spouse.** But, you may choose to enter -0- if you are married and have either a working spouse or more than one job. (This may help you avoid having too little tax withheld.) . . . . .   **C** _____

D   Enter number of **dependents** (other than your spouse or yourself) you will claim on your tax return . . .   **D** _____

E   Enter "1" if you will file as **head of household** on your tax return (see conditions under **Head of household** above)   .   **E** _____

F   Enter "1" if you have at least $1,500 of **child or dependent care expenses** for which you plan to claim a credit   . .   **F** _____

G   **Child Tax Credit:** • If your total income will be between $20,000 and $50,000 ($23,000 and $63,000 if married), enter "1" for each eligible child. • If your total income will be between $50,000 and $80,000 ($63,000 and $115,000 if married), enter "1" if you have two eligible children, enter "2" if you have three or four eligible children, or enter "3" if you have five or more eligible children   . .   **G** _____

H   Add lines A through G and enter total here. **Note:** This amount may be different from the number of exemptions you claim on your return.   ▶   **H** _____

For accuracy, complete all worksheets that apply.
- If you plan to **itemize or claim adjustments to income** and want to reduce your withholding, see the Deductions and Adjustments Worksheet on page 2.
- If you are **single,** have **more than one job** and your combined earnings from all jobs exceed $32,000, OR if you are **married** and have a **working spouse or more than one job** and the combined earnings from all jobs exceed $55,000, see the Two-Earner/Two-Job Worksheet on page 2 to avoid having too little tax withheld.
- If **neither** of the above situations applies, **stop here** and enter the number from line H on line 5 of Form W-4 below.

-----------------------   **Cut here and give the certificate to your employer. Keep the top part for your records.**   -----------------------

Form **W-4** Department of the Treasury Internal Revenue Service	**Employee's Withholding Allowance Certificate** ▶ **For Privacy Act and Paperwork Reduction Act Notice, see page 2.**	OMB No. 1545-0010 **1999**

1   Type or print your first name and middle initial   Last name | **2**   Your social security number

Home address (number and street or rural route)

3   ☐ Single ☐ Married ☐ Married, but withhold at higher Single rate.
Note: *If married, but legally separated, or spouse is a nonresident alien, check the Single box.*

City or town, state, and ZIP code

4   If your last name differs from that on your social security card, check here. **You** must call 1-800-772-1213 for a new card   . . . ▶ ☐

5   Total number of allowances you are claiming (from line H above or from the worksheets on page 2 if they apply)   .   **5** _____

6   Additional amount, if any, you want withheld from each paycheck   . . . .   **6** $ _____

7   I claim exemption from withholding for 1999, and I certify that I meet **BOTH** of the following conditions for exemption:
- Last year I had a right to a refund of **ALL** Federal income tax withheld because I had **NO** tax liability **AND**
- This year I expect a refund of **ALL** Federal income tax withheld because I expect to have **NO** tax liability.

If you meet both conditions, write "EXEMPT" here   . . . . ▶ **7** _____

Under penalties of perjury, I certify that I am entitled to the number of withholding allowances claimed on this certificate, or I am entitled to claim exempt status.

Employee's signature
(Form is not valid unless you sign it) ▶ _____   Date ▶ _____

8   Employer's name and address (Employer: Complete 8 and 10 only if sending to the IRS) | **9**   Office code (optional) | **10**   Employer identification number

Cat. No. 10220Q

W-4 FORM—PAGE 2

Form W-4 (1999)   Page **2**

Deductions and Adjustments Worksheet

Note: *Use this worksheet only if you plan to itemize deductions or claim adjustments to income on your 1999 tax return.*

1   Enter an estimate of your 1999 itemized deductions. These include qualifying home mortgage interest, charitable contributions, state and local taxes (but not sales taxes), medical expenses in excess of 7.5% of your income, and miscellaneous deductions. (For 1999, you may have to reduce your itemized deductions if your income is over $126,600 ($63,300 if married filing separately). Get Pub. 919 for details.)   **1** $ _____

2   Enter: { $7,200 if married filing jointly or qualifying widow(er) / $6,350 if head of household / $4,300 if single / $3,600 if married filing separately }   **2** $ _____

3   **Subtract** line 2 from line 1. If line 2 is greater than line 1, enter -0-   **3** $ _____

4   Enter an estimate of your 1999 adjustments to income, including alimony, deductible IRA contributions, and student loan interest   **4** $ _____

5   **Add** lines 3 and 4 and enter the total   **5** $ _____

6   Enter an estimate of your 1999 nonwage income (such as dividends or interest)   **6** $ _____

7   **Subtract** line 6 from line 5. Enter the result, but not less than -0-   **7** $ _____

8   **Divide** the amount on line 7 by $3,000 and enter the result here. Drop any fraction   **8**   _____

9   Enter the number from Personal Allowances Worksheet, line H, on page 1   **9**   _____

10   **Add** lines 8 and 9 and enter the total here. If you plan to use the Two-Earner/Two-Job Worksheet, also enter this total on line 1 below. Otherwise, **stop here** and enter this total on Form W-4, line 5, on page 1   **10**   _____

Two-Earner/Two-Job Worksheet

Note: *Use this worksheet only if the instructions for line H on page 1 direct you here.*

1   Enter the number from line H on page 1 (or from line 10 above if you used the Deductions and Adjustments Worksheet)   **1**   _____

2   Find the number in **Table 1** below that applies to the **LOWEST** paying job and enter it here   **2**   _____

3   If line 1 is **GREATER THAN OR EQUAL TO** line 2, subtract line 2 from line 1. Enter the result here (if zero, enter -0-) and on Form W-4, line 5, on page 1. **DO NOT** use the rest of this worksheet   **3**   _____

Note: *If line 1 is **LESS THAN** line 2, enter -0- on Form W-4, line 5, on page 1. Complete lines 4–9 to calculate the additional withholding amount necessary to avoid a year end tax bill.*

4   Enter the number from line 2 of this worksheet   **4**   _____

5   Enter the number from line 1 of this worksheet   **5**   _____

6   **Subtract** line 5 from line 4   **6**   _____

7   Find the amount in **Table 2** below that applies to the **HIGHEST** paying job and enter it here   **7** $ _____

8   **Multiply** line 7 by line 6 and enter the result here. This is the additional annual withholding amount needed   **8** $ _____

9   Divide line 8 by the number of pay periods remaining in 1999. (For example, divide by 26 if you are paid every other week and you complete this form in December 1998.) Enter the result here and on Form W-4, line 6, page 1. This is the additional amount to be withheld from each paycheck   **9** $ _____

Table 1: Two-Earner/Two-Job Worksheet

Married Filing Jointly				All Others			
If wages from **LOWEST** paying job are—	Enter on line 2 above	If wages from **LOWEST** paying job are—	Enter on line 2 above	If wages from **LOWEST** paying job are—	Enter on line 2 above	If wages from **LOWEST** paying job are—	Enter on line 2 above
$0 - $4,000	0	40,001 - 45,000	8	$0 - $5,000	0	65,001 - 80,000	8
4,001 - 7,000	1	45,001 - 54,000	9	5,001 - 11,000	1	80,001 - 100,000	9
7,001 - 12,000	2	54,001 - 62,000	10	11,001 - 16,000	2	100,001 and over	10
12,001 - 18,000	3	62,001 - 70,000	11	16,001 - 21,000	3		
18,001 - 24,000	4	70,001 - 85,000	12	21,001 - 25,000	4		
24,001 - 28,000	5	85,001 - 100,000	13	25,001 - 40,000	5		
28,001 - 35,000	6	100,001 - 110,000	14	40,001 - 50,000	6		
35,001 - 40,000	7	110,001 and over	15	50,001 - 65,000	7		

Table 2: Two-Earner/Two-Job Worksheet

Married Filing Jointly		All Others	
If wages from **HIGHEST** paying job are—	Enter on line 7 above	If wages from **HIGHEST** paying job are—	Enter on line 7 above
$0 - $50,000	$400	$0 - $30,000	$400
50,001 - 100,000	770	30,001 - 60,000	770
100,001 - 130,000	850	60,001 - 120,000	850
130,001 - 240,000	1,000	120,001 - 250,000	1,000
240,001 and over	1,100	250,000 and over	1,100

W-4 FORM—ACTIVITY 1

> **ACTIVITY:** Have students complete the W-4 form for Joe Hernandez as described in the student activity text. Ask them to assume that Joe does not want additional tax withheld and that he will claim only an allowance for himself. Tell them not to enter "exempt" for number 7 and to ignore sections 8, 9, and 10.
>
> If your class includes students from other countries, make sure they practice filling out the name, address, and Social Security number.

Describe taxpayer

Joe Hernandez is single and has no dependents. He does not want any additional amount withheld. He lives at 300 Primavera Street, Apt. A, Impuesto, CA 90000. His Social Security number is 123-45-6789.

NOTE: For your convenience, a completed W-4 form is included here.

- - - - - - - - - - - - - -   **Cut here and give the certificate to your employer. Keep the top part for your records.**   - - - - - - - - - - - - - -

Form **W-4**	**Employee's Withholding Allowance Certificate**	OMB No. 1545-0010
Department of the Treasury Internal Revenue Service	► **For Privacy Act and Paperwork Reduction Act Notice, see page 2.**	1999

1 Type or print your first name and middle initial **Joe**	Last name **Hernandez**	2 Your social security number **123 45 6789**
Home address (number and street or rural route) **300 Primavera St. Apt. A**	3 ☒ Single ☐ Married ☐ Married, but withhold at higher Single rate. **Note:** *If married, but legally separated, or spouse is a nonresident alien, check the Single box.*	
City or town, state, and ZIP code **Impuesto, CA 90000**	4 If your last name differs from that on your social security card, check here. **You** must call 1-800-772-1213 for a new card . . ► ☐	

5	Total number of allowances you are claiming (from line H above or from the worksheets on page 2 if they apply) .	5	1
6	Additional amount, if any, you want withheld from each paycheck	6	$

7   I claim exemption from withholding for 1999, and I certify that I meet **BOTH** of the following conditions for exemption:
- Last year I had a right to a refund of **ALL** Federal income tax withheld because I had **NO** tax liability **AND**
- This year I expect a refund of **ALL** Federal income tax withheld because I expect to have **NO** tax liability.

If you meet both conditions, write "EXEMPT" here . . . . ► | 7 |

Under penalties of perjury, I certify that I am entitled to the number of withholding allowances claimed on this certificate, or I am entitled to claim exempt status.

Employee's signature
(Form is not valid
unless you sign it) ►   Date ►

8 Employer's name and address (Employer: Complete 8 and 10 only if sending to the IRS)	9 Office code (optional)	10 Employer identification number

Cat. No. 10220Q

W-4 FORM—ACTIVITY 2

> **ACTIVITY:** Have students complete the W-4 form for Kim Tranh as described in the student activity text. Ask them to assume that Kim does not want additional tax withheld. Tell them not to enter "exempt" for number 7 and to ignore sections 8, 9, and 10.
>
> If your class includes students from other countries, make sure they practice filling out the name, address, and Social Security number.

Describe taxpayer

Kim Tranh is married and has two children. She and her husband will claim a total of four allowances. She will claim two on her W-4 form, and her husband will claim two on his. She does not want any additional amount withheld. She lives at 4300 Lakeview Avenue, Midville, TX 70000. Her Social Security number is 987-65-4321.

NOTE: For your convenience, a completed W-4 form is included here.

- **Cut here and give the certificate to your employer. Keep the top part for your records.** -

Form **W-4**	**Employee's Withholding Allowance Certificate**	OMB No. 1545-0010
Department of the Treasury Internal Revenue Service	▶ **For Privacy Act and Paperwork Reduction Act Notice, see page 2.**	1999

1 Type or print your first name and middle initial **Kim**	Last name **Tranh**	2 Your social security number **987 65 4321**

Home address (number and street or rural route) **4300 Lakeview Avenue**	3 ☐ Single ☒ Married ☐ Married, but withhold at higher Single rate. **Note:** *If married, but legally separated, or spouse is a nonresident alien, check the Single box.*
City or town, state, and ZIP code **Midville, TX 70000**	4 If your last name differs from that on your social security card, check here. **You** must call 1-800-772-1213 for a new card . . . ▶ ☐

5	Total number of allowances you are claiming (from line H above or from the worksheets on page 2 if they apply) .	5	**2**
6	Additional amount, if any, you want withheld from each paycheck	6	$

7 I claim exemption from withholding for 1999, and I certify that I meet **BOTH** of the following conditions for exemption:
- Last year I had a right to a refund of **ALL** Federal income tax withheld because I had **NO** tax liability **AND**
- This year I expect a refund of **ALL** Federal income tax withheld because I expect to have **NO** tax liability.

If you meet both conditions, write "EXEMPT" here . . . . ▶ | 7 |

Under penalties of perjury, I certify that I am entitled to the number of withholding allowances claimed on this certificate, or I am entitled to claim exempt status.

Employee's signature
(Form is not valid
unless you sign it) ▶   Date ▶

8 Employer's name and address (Employer: Complete 8 and 10 only if sending to the IRS)	9 Office code (optional)	10 Employer identification number

Cat. No. 10220Q

SAMPLE PAY STUBS

Discuss pay stubs

Employers usually provide some kind of record of the amount the employee was paid and how much money was withheld. This is usually called a "pay stub."

Pay stubs from different employers look different. Some pay stubs show only the information for the current pay period. Some also show the year to date (YTD).

Sometimes money is deducted from the paycheck in addition to withholding for taxes. Deductions may be taken for union dues, pension plans, and health insurance, among other things.

Review gross pay

Gross pay is the total amount of pay you earn before your employer withholds federal and state taxes.

Review net pay

Net pay is the amount of pay you receive after your employer withholds federal and state taxes.

Ask questions

1. Does pay stub A show the current pay period only, or does it include year-to-date amounts?

   Includes year to date.

2. How much does Joe Hernandez earn per hour?

   $8.93

3. How many hours did Joe Hernandez work during the pay period?

   80 hours

4. How much does Kim Tranh earn per hour?

   $6.09

5. How many hours did Kim Tranh work during the pay period?

   48 hours

ACTIVITY: Have students look at their own pay stubs to determine if similar information is shown.

NOTE: If you have undocumented workers in your class, you should be aware that some employers do not provide them with pay stubs. The employers may not send withholding to the government. This is a sensitive issue. Current law requires employers to withhold taxes and send the taxes to the government. It also prohibits the hiring of undocumented workers.

WITHHOLDING ACTIVITY

ACTIVITY: Have students look at the sample pay stubs. Students may also use their own pay stubs. For each one, students fill in the items listed in the table for the current pay period.

- Salary or gross pay.
- Federal income tax withheld.
- State income tax withheld.
- Social Security tax withheld.
- Medicare tax withheld.
- Other withheld (if applicable).
- Net pay (take-home pay).

Ask volunteers to give their answers out loud, and ask the class if they agree. You may also ask students to fill in the amounts for the year to date.

CHAPTER 4

Filing Concepts and Deadlines

OVERVIEW

Topics

- Your filing status
- Who must file
- Dependents
- Filing if not required
- What happens when you file
- What happens if you make a mistake
- Penalties
- Deadlines
- Social Security numbers
- Individual Taxpayer Identification Numbers (ITINs)

Objectives

By the end of this chapter, the students will be able to:

- Determine their own filing status.
- Explain who should file.
- State who can qualify as a dependent.
- Describe penalties.
- Identify the deadline for filing the tax return.
- Explain who needs a Social Security number and how to get one.

Student activities

- Determine their filing status.
- List their dependents.
- Take a true/false quiz.

- Fill in a crossword puzzle.
- Complete an "alphabet soup" word search.

Things you need

- It may be useful to have a copy of Publication 17 or instructions for Form 1040EZ or 1040A.

Important points

- The concepts of filing status and dependents are essential, but they may be difficult for students to understand because of a number of special circumstances defined by the IRS. Concentrate on the main points, but be aware that these special circumstances exist and that they may apply to a few students. Refer students to the instructions in the form or Publication 17. Mention resources described in the final chapter of the workbook.

FILING CONCEPTS AND DEADLINES

In this chapter, you will learn about:

- **Your filing status.**
  Special categories to define your family situation for tax purposes.

- **Who must file.**
  Depending on your age and income, you might be required to file taxes.

- **Dependents.**
  People who are supported by others.

- **Filing if not required.**

  In many cases, there may be benefits of filing, even if it is not required.

- **What happens when you file.**

  You will either owe money or receive a refund.

- **What happens if you make a mistake or don't file.**

  If you make a mistake, you can file an amended return. If you don't file, there are serious penalties you will face.

- **Deadlines.**

  The deadline for your income tax return form is April 15.

- **Social Security numbers.**

- **Individual Taxpayer Identification Numbers (ITINs).**

VOCABULARY

> **ACTIVITY:** Before providing the definitions, ask for volunteers to define each word. Write brief definitions on a transparency or on the blackboard, or send volunteers to the board to record their definitions, and have the class refine the sentence structure and spelling of each. In addition, you can have the students use each word in a sentence.

filing status: How you define your family situation for tax purposes. You must use one of the special IRS categories.

head of household: Special filing status for single people who support certain relatives. The head of household filing status is often used by a single person with children.

support: Paying for such things as rent, food, clothes, medical expenses, and educational expenses for another person. Parents usually support their children.

widow/widower: Person whose spouse has died. *Widow* refers to a woman; *widower* refers to a man. For tax purposes, it is a special filing status.

dependent: Person who is financially supported by someone else; usually a child.

earned income credit: A special credit for low-income parents who earned less than a certain amount. More than $3,000 may be received for this credit.

penalty: A fine for not following IRS rules. Usually, the IRS charges you extra money if you send in your income tax forms late or if you do not pay all of the tax money that you owe. In very serious cases, such as fraud, penalties may include going to jail.

audit: A check of your tax return by the IRS. The IRS is looking for mistakes.

deadline: Last date by which tax returns should be completed and mailed to the IRS.

> **ACTIVITY:** Have students circle the first instance of each word in the chapter.

WHAT IS YOUR FILING STATUS?

Describe filing status

Your filing status is how you define your family situation for tax purposes. You must use one of the categories listed in your workbook. These categories are defined by the IRS.

- ☐ **Single person**

  A single individual or a divorced individual.

☐ **Head of household**

An unmarried person who shared and maintained a home for himself/herself and a qualifying relative for more than six months. Examples of qualifying relatives are children, in-laws, grandparents, grandchildren, brother, and sister.

An unmarried person who maintained the main home for a parent for the whole year. The parent and unmarried person may live in separate homes.

A married person who is separated AND who supported himself/herself and a son or a daughter in a shared home for more than six months AND who lived apart from the spouse during the last six months of the filing year AND who files a separate tax return.

☐ **Widow or widower with dependent child**

A widow or widower who has not remarried AND whose spouse died during the previous two years AND who has at least one dependent child.

For example, for 1998 returns, the taxpayer is a widow(er) if the spouse died anytime in 1996 or 1997.

☐ **Married couple, filing together (jointly)**

A married couple.

A person who became a widow or widower during the filing year.

☐ **Married couple, filing separately**

A married couple who file separate returns. Each spouse filing separately is charged at a higher rate than if the couple filed together.

ACTIVITY: Ask students to place a check by their filing status.

WHO MUST FILE?

Summarize need to file

Everyone who has earnings or income must determine if they should file an income tax return. Most workers have a portion of their paychecks withheld to pay an estimate of their taxes. The tax return is used to calculate the exact tax bill (see Chapter 3).

Most, but not all, people who have income are required by law to file a tax return.

Discuss who must file

For the 1998 tax year, you had to file if you were in one of the following groups:

Age	Who earned more than
☐ Single persons	
Under 65	$6,950.00
65 or over	$8,000.00
☐ Heads of households	
Under 65	$8,950.00
65 or over	$10,000.00
☐ Married persons, filing together (jointly)	
Both under 65	$12,500.00
One under 65, one 65 or over	$13,350.00
Both 65 or over	$14,200.00
☐ Married persons, filing separately	
Any age	$2,700.00
☐ Widows or widowers with dependent child	
Under 65	$9,800.00
65 or over	$10,650.00

NOTE: You may wish to update the figures for the current year by consulting instructions on the current tax form or Publication 17.

ACTIVITY: Tell students to place a check next to the category that applies to them. Explain that if none of these categories applies, they are probably not required to file an income tax return.

Ask questions

1. Does the IRS consider you a widow if you have a dependent child, you have not remarried, and your husband died five years ago?

   No. You are considered a head of household.

2. If you are not married and have two dependent children, are you considered single by the IRS?

   No. You are considered a head of household.

3. Are you required to file a tax return if you are married, you and your spouse are over 65, and you earned $14,000.00?

   No. You are under the limit of $14,200.00.

4. If you are a head of household under 65 and you earned only $9,000, are you required to file?

   Yes. You are over the limit of $8,950.00.

5. Are married workers required to file if they earned $20,000?

   Yes. They are over all of the limits.

WHO IS A DEPENDENT?

Describe dependents

People who are supported by others are generally considered dependents. If you have children or other people you support, you can claim them as dependents on your form. You get a deduction for each dependent.

Five requirements must be met to qualify as a dependent.

- **The person filing the tax form must provide more than half of the support of the dependent.**

  Support includes rent, food, clothes, medical expenses, educational expenses, and so on.

- **The dependent cannot earn more than $2,700.00.**

  This does not apply to your child under age 19 or your child who is a full-time student under age 24.

- **The dependent must live for the entire year with the person filing the income tax return unless she or he is a relative, for example:**

  Son, daughter, grandchild, parent, grandparent, brother, sister, brother-in-law, sister-in-law, mother-in-law, father-in-law, and (if related by blood) uncle, aunt, niece, or nephew.

  If the dependent is a cousin, he or she must live in the taxpayer's home.

- **The dependent must be a resident of the United States, Canada, or Mexico.**

  This includes U.S. citizens, resident aliens, and residents of Mexico or Canada.

- **If the dependent is married, he or she must not file a joint income tax return with his or her spouse.**

NOTE: If the students have a potentially complex situation, such as support of family members other than children, refer them to the tax form instructions, Publication 17, or the resources in Chapter 8.

WHO ARE YOUR DEPENDENTS?

ACTIVITY: Have students list all of their dependents. Tell them to make certain that each dependent meets all five requirements.

---

1. _____   4. _____

2. _____   5. _____

3. _____   6. _____

NOTE: A spouse who does not earn income is not considered a dependent. He or she files a joint return with the employed spouse. Both spouses get an exemption.

SHOULD YOU FILE IF NOT REQUIRED?

Discuss filing

Sometimes it is a good idea to file a tax return even if you are not required to do so. You should file if:

- **You had income tax withheld from your pay.**

    You may get a refund.

- **You qualify for the earned income credit.**

    This is a refundable credit of up to $3,756.00.

- **Your income must be less than $30,095.00**

    If the credit is larger than your tax, the difference will be refunded to you.

NOTE: Students may wish to file so that they can document their earnings or their residence in the United States.

One important reason to fill out a form is to determine if you will receive money back. If, after filling out a form, you find that you will not get any money back, you do not have to file if you are not required to.

WHAT HAPPENS WHEN YOU FILE?

Describe possibilities

Usually, when you file, one of two things will happen.

- **You will get money back.**

    The refund check will come in the mail, or you can request to have your refund check deposited directly to your bank account.

    If you do not get your refund within eight weeks, call the IRS.

    OR

- **You will owe more money to pay your taxes.**

    Pay the amount you owe when you send in your tax return form.

Emphasize payment

If you cannot pay the whole amount, send in the tax return form on time with a partial payment. The IRS will bill you for the balance, plus interest.

Discuss changing W-4

If you get a lot of money back, or if you owe a lot of money, you should think about changing the amount of money withheld from what you earn.

- **To do this, submit a new W-4 form to your employer. (See Chapter 3.)**

NOTE: Some tax preparation services provide an instant refund. However, the taxpayer must usually pay a fee or interest for this service.

WHAT IF YOU MAKE A MISTAKE?

Explain amended returns

- If after you file you find out you made a mistake, you can file an amended return. This is a separate form that you use to correct the mistake.

- You can even use the amended return to get more money back if you find that your mistake means that you overpaid your taxes. However, the IRS will not pay you interest on any money you overpaid.

Describe audits

- The IRS may audit your tax return. This means that the IRS reviews your income tax return. If the IRS finds a mistake, you

may have to pay more taxes, plus interest. Sometimes there is also a penalty.

- The IRS audits only a small percentage of tax returns.

PENALTIES FOR NOT FILING OR FOR MISTAKES

Identify civil penalties

You may have to pay civil penalties if you:

- Are required to file a return and don't file.
- File late.
- Don't pay enough taxes.
- Make serious mistakes.
- Commit fraud.

Describe penalties

These penalties are extra payments, in addition to taxes and interest.

Discuss criminal penalties

If you commit serious fraud, you may be brought to trial. In addition to making penalty payments, you could be sent to jail.

NOTE: Tax liabilities can never be eliminated, even if a person declares bankruptcy. The IRS can also take money from bank accounts and from wages. Sometimes the IRS has amnesty programs that make it easier for people who owe taxes from previous years to pay.

It is important to understand that consequences can be severe if a taxpayer is caught cheating or making serious mistakes.

DEADLINES

Identify deadlines

The deadline for filing your income tax return form is:

- **April 15.**

  Or the following Monday if April 15 falls on a weekend.

- **Your form must be postmarked no later than April 15.**

  Some post offices stay open late on April 15.

- **Don't wait until the last minute!**

Discuss filing early or in April

Generally, most people who are going to get a refund file their tax return early. That way they receive their money sooner.

Many people who will owe additional taxes file their return at the deadline so they can keep their money longer.

It is a good idea to have your tax return finished early so you know if you are going to get a refund or owe additional taxes.

Discuss extensions

You can get a filing extension if you need one.

- An automatic four-month filing extension is granted if you complete and send Form 4868 by April 15.

- If you owe money, you must pay the amount when you file Form 4868. This means that you still have to pay all the taxes you owe by April 15, even if you don't file. If you had enough money withheld from your paychecks, this is not a problem.

- If you are going to receive a refund, you will get it later if you use an extension.

- Usually, extensions are used by people with complicated tax situations.

Additional extension

You can get another extension by filing Form 2688. You must already have filed Form 4868 on time. You must also state the reason for the extension. The IRS can reject this additional extension. It is not automatic like the first one.

SOCIAL SECURITY NUMBERS

Introduce topic

We have discussed many of the concepts you need to know about filing an income tax return. It is important to understand that the taxpayers and their dependents must have Social Security numbers to file the tax return.

Ask and explain

What is a Social Security number?

It is a number used to record your Social Security contributions while you are working and to record the payments you get when you receive benefits (for example, when you retire).

The format of the Social Security number is always:

- 000-00-0000

> **ACTIVITY:** Ask students if they know their Social Security numbers. Have students write down their number in the student activity text under the zeros.

Ask and explain

Who needs a Social Security number?

- Anyone who files a tax return form.

- Dependents (for example, your children).

Ask and explain

Where do you get a Social Security number?

- File a Form SS-5 with your local Social Security Administration office.

- Call the office to find out what documentation you need to prove your age, identity, and citizenship.

- You can use the Internet to get information about Social Security: www.ssa.gov

---

ACTIVITY: If your students could benefit by practicing their communications skills, use a role-play exercise to have students simulate calling the office to find out what documentation they need to get a Social Security number. Pair up the students, and have half act as the Social Security administrator and half as the caller. Then switch. Alternatively, you can act as the Social Security administrator.

SAMPLE FORM SS-5

Describe form

- Your student activity text contains a sample of the form used to apply for a Social Security Number Card. This form is used to apply for an individual's original card, or if the person needs to get a replacement or make a correction.

ACTIVITY: If students need practice filling out forms, lead them through the form and have them fill it out.

FORM SS-5

SOCIAL SECURITY ADMINISTRATION Application for a Social Security Card

Form Approved
OMB No. 0960-0066

		First	Full Middle Name	Last
1	**NAME** TO BE SHOWN ON CARD ➜			
	FULL NAME AT BIRTH IF OTHER THAN ABOVE ➜	First	Full Middle Name	Last
	OTHER NAMES USED ➜			

2 MAILING ADDRESS Do Not Abbreviate ➜

Street Address, Apt. No., PO Box, Rural Route No.

City	State	Zip Code

3 CITIZENSHIP (Check One) ➜

☐ U.S. Citizen ☐ Legal Alien Allowed To Work ☐ Legal Alien **Not** Allowed To Work ☐ Other (See Instructions On Page 1)

4 SEX ➜ ☐ Male ☐ Female

5 RACE/ETHNIC DESCRIPTION (Check One Only–Voluntary) ➜

☐ Asian Asian-American or Pacific Islander ☐ Hispanic ☐ Black (Not Hispanic) ☐ North American Indian or Alaskan Native ☐ White (Not Hispanic)

6 DATE OF BIRTH Month, Day, Year

7 PLACE OF BIRTH (Do Not Abbreviate) City State or Foreign Country FCI

Office Use Only

8 A. MOTHER'S MAIDEN NAME ➜ First Full Middle Name Last Name At Her Birth

B. MOTHER'S SOCIAL SECURITY NUMBER (Complete only if applying for a number for a child under age 18.) ➜ ☐☐☐–☐☐–☐☐☐☐

9 A. FATHER'S NAME ➜ First Full Middle Name Last

B. FATHER'S SOCIAL SECURITY NUMBER (Complete only if applying for a number for a child under age 18.) ➜ ☐☐☐–☐☐–☐☐☐☐

10 Has the applicant or anyone acting on his/her behalf ever filed for or received a Social Security number card before?

☐ Yes (If "yes," answer questions 11-13.) ☐ No (If "no," go on to question 14.) ☐ Don't Know (If "don't know," go on to question 14.)

11 Enter the Social Security number previously assigned to the person listed in item 1. ➜ ☐☐☐–☐☐–☐☐☐☐

12 Enter the name shown on the most recent Social Security card issued for the person listed in item 1. ➜ First Middle Last

13 Enter any different date of birth if used on an earlier application for a card. ➜ Month, Day, Year

14 TODAY'S DATE Month, Day, Year

15 DAYTIME PHONE NUMBER (   ) Area Code Number

DELIBERATELY FURNISHING (OR CAUSING TO BE FURNISHED) FALSE INFORMATION ON THIS APPLICATION IS A CRIME PUNISHABLE BY FINE OR IMPRISONMENT, OR BOTH.

16 YOUR SIGNATURE ▶

17 YOUR RELATIONSHIP TO THE PERSON IN ITEM 1 IS:
☐ Self ☐ Natural or Adoptive Parent ☐ Legal Guardian ☐ Other (Specify)

DO NOT WRITE BELOW THIS LINE (FOR SSA USE ONLY)

NPN			DOC	NTI	CAN		ITV
PBC	EVI	EVA	EVC	PRA	NWR	DNR	UNIT

EVIDENCE SUBMITTED

SIGNATURE AND TITLE OF EMPLOYEE(S) REVIEWING EVIDENCE AND/OR CONDUCTING INTERVIEW

DATE

DCL DATE

INDIVIDUAL TAXPAYER IDENTIFICATION NUMBERS (ITINs)

Introduce topic

Sometimes taxpayers or their dependents are not eligible to apply for a Social Security number and they cannot submit an SS-5.

Ask and explain

What can these taxpayers or their dependents do?

- They can fill out a W-7 form to apply for an individual taxpayer identification number, or ITIN.

  This is a special form created by the IRS for taxpayers or their dependents who are not eligible to apply for a Social Security number. By completing this form, taxpayers or their dependents will receive an Individual Taxpayer Identification Number (ITIN). The ITIN is a nine-digit number that can be substituted for the Social Security number on the income tax return.

- The ITIN is only good for filing income tax. It cannot be used at work.

Ask and explain

Where do you get an Individual Taxpayer Identification Number?

- File a form W-7 with your local IRS.
- Call the office to find out what documentation you need to submit with the W-7.

Describe form

Your student activity text contains a sample of the form used to apply for an Individual Taxpayer Identification Number.

> **ACTIVITY:** If students need practice filling out forms, lead them through the form and have them fill it out.

Form **W-7**
(Rev. February 1998)

Department of the Treasury
Internal Revenue Service

Application for IRS Individual Taxpayer Identification Number
▶ See instructions.   ▶ Please type or print.
▶ **For use by individuals who are NOT U.S. citizens, nationals, or permanent residents.**

OMB No. 1545-1483

Please note the following when completing this form:
- *This number is for tax purposes only.* **Do not submit** *this form if you have, or are eligible to obtain, a U.S. social security number (SSN).*
- *Receipt of an ITIN creates no inference regarding your immigration status or your right to work in the United States.*
- *Receipt of an ITIN does not make you eligible to claim the earned income credit (EIC).*

FOR IRS USE ONLY

Reason you are submitting Form W-7. (Check only one box. See instructions.)

a ☐ Nonresident alien required to obtain ITIN to claim tax treaty benefit

b ☐ Nonresident alien filing a U.S. tax return and not eligible for an SSN

c ☐ U.S. resident alien (based on days present in the United States) filing a U.S. tax return and not eligible for an SSN

d ☐ Dependent of U.S. person } Enter name and SSN of U.S. person (see instructions) ▶ _ _ _ _ _ _ _ _ _ _ _ _ _ _ _

e ☐ Spouse of U.S. person

f ☐ Other (specify) _

1 Name
(see instructions)
Name at birth if different . . ▶

1a Last name (surname or family name)	First name	Middle name
1b Last name (surname or family name)	First name	Middle name

2 Permanent residence address, if any
(see instructions)

Street address, apartment number, or rural route number. **Do not use a P.O. box number.**

City or town, state or province, and country. Include ZIP code or postal code where appropriate.

3 Mailing address
(if different from above)

Street address, apartment number, P.O. box number, or rural route number.

City or town, state or province, and country. Include ZIP code or postal code where appropriate.

4 Birth information

Date of birth (month, day, year) / /	Country of birth	City and state or province (optional)	**5** ☐ Male ☐ Female

6 Family information
(see instructions)

Father's last name (surname)	First name	Middle name
Mother's maiden name (surname)	First name	Middle name

7 Other information

7a Country(ies) of citizenship	7b Foreign tax identification number	7c Type of U.S. visa (if any) and expiration date

7d Describe identification document(s) submitted (see instructions).

☐ Passport   ☐ Driver's license/State I.D.   ☐ INS documentation   ☐ Other _ _ _ _ _ _ _ _
Issued by: Number:

7e Have you previously received a U.S. temporary Taxpayer Identification Number (TIN) or Employer Identification Number (EIN)?
☐ **No/Do not know.** Skip line 7f.
☐ **Yes.** Complete line 7f. If you need more space, list on a sheet and attach to this form. (See instructions.)

7f **TIN** ☐☐☐-☐☐-☐☐☐☐   **EIN** ☐-☐ ☐☐☐☐☐☐☐

Enter the name under which the TIN was issued.   Enter the name under which the EIN was issued.

Sign Here

Keep a copy of this form for your records.

Under penalties of perjury, I (applicant/delegate/acceptance agent) declare that I have examined this application, including accompanying documentation and statements, and to the best of my knowledge and belief, it is true, correct, and complete. I authorize the IRS to disclose to my acceptance agent returns or return information necessary to resolve matters regarding the assignment of my IRS individual taxpayer identification number (ITIN).

▶ Signature of applicant (if delegate, see instructions)	Date (month, day, year) / /	Phone number
▶ Name of delegate, if applicable (type or print)	Delegate's relationship to applicant ▶	☐ Parent ☐ Guardian

Acceptance Agent's Use ONLY

▶ Signature	Date (month, day, year) / /	Phone: ( ) FAX: ( )
▶ Name and title (type or print)	Name of company	EIN

For Paperwork Reduction Act Notice, see page 4.   Cat. No. 10229L   Form **W-7** (Rev. 2-98)

TRUE OR FALSE

ACTIVITY: Have students complete the true–false exercise by writing **T** for statements that are true and **F** for statements that are false.

NOTE: Answers are included here for your convenience.

Answer Key

1. __F__ The filing status of a person with a small child but no spouse is "single."

2. __T__ If you owe taxes you are required to pay them by April 15.

3. __T__ An aunt may be considered your dependent even if she doesn't live with you, if she meets all the other requirements.

4. __F__ Tips are not considered income that can be taxed.

5. __T__ Withholding is money your employer takes from your pay and sends to the government to pay an estimate of your total tax bill.

6. __T__ Your federal income taxes are used to help pay for health and education programs.

7. __F__ If your employer withheld money from your paycheck, you never have to file a tax return form.

8. __F__ Social Security tax is the same as federal income tax.

9. __T__ Even if you don't have enough money to pay all your taxes, you should file on time and pay part of your taxes.

10. __F__ Only paid workers in a family need Social Security numbers.

CROSSWORD PUZZLE

ACTIVITY: Have students complete the crossword puzzle.

NOTE: A completed puzzle is included here for your convenience.

Across

2.   The money you pay to the government is income _____ .

5.   If you are not married, you are _____ .

6.   The W-4 form tells your employer how much money to take out, or _____ , from your pay.

7.   The agency responsible for income tax is the _____ .

9.   Your young child who lives with you is your _____ .

10.   The money you receive for work is one type of _____ .

Down

1.   Another word for wages or salaries is _____ .

3.   A woman whose husband has died is a _____ .

4.   You must file your tax return by the _____ or pay a penalty.

8.   The deadline for filing your tax return form is in the month of _____ .

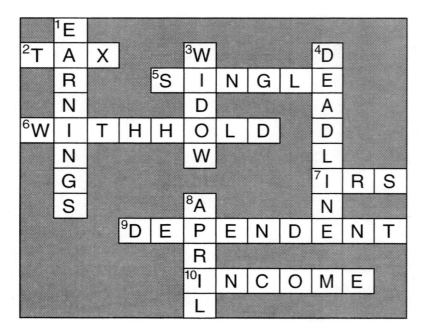

ALPHABET SOUP

ACTIVITY: Have students find and circle each of the words listed in the workbook.

NOTE: A completed puzzle is included here for your convenience. "Report" occurs twice in the grid.

Answer Key

```
H  P  Z  Y  I  W  X  M  D  A  E  T  G  N  O  Q
B  I  J  L  T  K  R  C  S  P  Z  U  V  K  F  C
F  W  A  G  E  S  S  U  P  P  O  R  T  J  Y  D
J  I  U  F  M  E  X  T  E  N  S  I  O  N  P  M
O  F  M  D  I  W  E  X  E  M  P  T  I  O  N  X
D  E  H  N  Z  O  P  E  N  A  L  T  Y  P  G  I
H  A  E  I  E  D  E  D  U  C  T  I  O  N  R  L
S  T  A  N  D  A  R  D  E  M  E  F  R  C  M  C
C  A  D  T  E  N  S  E  P  A  R  A  T  E  L  Y
G  X  O  E  F  S  O  C  I  A  L  W  A  D  M  O
W  T  F  R  Y  J  N  K  X  G  B  I  D  L  A  H
A  A  H  E  U  M  A  R  R  I  E  D  K  Z  T  Q
N  B  O  S  K  T  L  O  N  G  F  O  R  M  N  J
E  L  U  T  P  F  K  X  F  V  I  W  E  J  W  Q
T  E  S  I  N  G  L  E  D  L  L  E  P  H  U  K
R  S  E  R  E  P  O  R  T  U  E  R  O  C  M  T
X  U  H  A  B  I  R  S  G  J  M  Q  R  D  A  P
Q  M  O  Y  C  S  E  C  U  R  I  T  Y  Y  D
P  E  L  I  B  R  A  R  Y  B  C  R  N  C  O  M
Y  L  D  E  P  E  N  D  E  N  T  W  G  J  X  Z
```

deduction	interest	personal	standard
dependent	itemize	report	support
exemption	library	security	tax tables
extension	long form	separately	wages
file	married	single	widower
head of household	penalty	social	wife

QUESTIONS

> **ACTIVITY:** Have students answer the following questions. Answers are included here for your reference.

1. If Marilyn Johnson is divorced and has a child living with her, what is her filing status?

   Head of household. She is not single because she has a child.

2. If Marco Santillana's wife died three years ago, and he has one six-year-old daughter, what is his filing status?

   Head of household. For tax purposes, he is not a widower because his wife died more than two years ago.

3. Stella and Victor Goldstein are both 35 years old, are married, and have one child. She earned $5,000 and he earned $15,500. Are they required to file a tax return?

   Yes. They are married persons who earned more than the minimum.

4. Rachel Hollander is 75 and lives alone. Her husband died five years ago. She earned $8,230. Is she required to file a tax return?

   Yes. She is a single person who earned more than the minimum. For tax purposes, she is not a widow because her husband died more than two years ago and she does not have a dependent child.

5. Bob Deauville is a 17-year-old unmarried high school student. He works part-time at a fast-food restaurant. He earned $4,600. Does he have to file a tax return? If so, what is his filing status? Can he still be claimed as a dependent by his parents?

   Bob does not have to file because he earns less than the minimum. He wants to file because he had tax withheld and he wants a refund. He would file as a single taxpayer using the 1040EZ. His parents could still claim him as a dependent on their tax return because children under 19 may earn any amount of income and still be claimed as dependents on the parents' tax return.

CHAPTER 5

Filing Procedures

OVERVIEW

Topics

- Basic filing procedures
- Calculating your total income
- Standard deduction
- Itemized deductions
- IRA deductions
- Exemptions
- Deductions
- Tax tables
- Tax credits
- Forms you need to file your income tax return
- Information you need to fill out the forms
- Review of filing procedure

Objectives

By the end of this chapter, the students will be able to:

- Explain basic filing procedures.
- Calculate total income using W-2 and 1099 forms.
- Describe deductions and exemptions.
- Use tax tables.
- Explain tax credits.
- List forms needed to file the tax return.
- List the information needed to fill out the forms.

Student activities

- Read W-2 forms and write down amounts withheld.
- Look up taxable income in tax tables.
- Perform an exercise in calculating income tax.

Things you need

- You may wish to use current tax tables.
- You may also wish to tell students the current amounts for deductions, exemptions, credits, etc. You will find this information in Publication 17.
- Students may wish to refer to their own W-2 forms during the W-2 form activity.
- It may be useful to write the basic filing procedures on the board or a flip chart page so you can refer to it during the discussion of each point.

Important points

- The basic tax calculation exercise is designed to allow the students to practice the process of calculating taxes without the tax return forms. This will enable them to understand the concepts behind the process before they approach the forms.

FILING PROCEDURES

Describe chapter

In this chapter, you will learn about:

- **Basic filing procedures**

  This will give you an overview of the procedures for working with the tax return form. Once you understand the basic concepts, it will be easier to work with the forms. We will discuss each procedure step by step.

- **Calculating your total income**

  The first step is to calculate your total income. To do this, you need to be able to read the W-2 and 1099-INT forms you will receive in the mail.

- **Deductions and exemptions**

  You are allowed to subtract certain amounts from your income. These amounts are not taxed.

- **Tax tables**

  To figure your total taxes, you must look up your taxable income in the tax tables.

- **Tax credits**

  You may be able to subtract an amount from the taxes you owe; this is a tax credit.

- **Forms you need to file your income tax return**

  Different forms are used for filing tax returns. We will discuss each one.

- **Information you need to fill out the forms**

  We will list the information you will need before you can complete your tax return.

Before we go any further, let's discuss the vocabulary for this chapter.

VOCABULARY

> **ACTIVITY:** Before providing the definitions, ask for volunteers to define each word. Write brief definitions on a transparency or on the blackboard, or send volunteers to the board to record their definitions, and have the class refine the sentence structure and spelling of each. Have the students use each word in a sentence.

wages: Money you are paid by your employer; your salary.

interest: Money a bank pays you for savings you have deposited there. You must report the interest you receive on your tax return forms. (You pay interest to the bank if you have a loan.)

standard deduction: A fixed amount of money that the government allows you to subtract from the income you report to the IRS. The amount varies according to your filing status.

itemized deduction: The actual amount of approved expenditures you may subtract from your income. Use this amount only if it is larger than the standard deduction.

exemption: Amount of money you are allowed to subtract from your income for each dependent. You are allowed an exemption for yourself if you support yourself. Your spouse is also allowed an exemption.

IRA: Individual retirement account. IRAs are special savings accounts for workers who may or may not have a pension or retirement plan at work.

W-2 form: The form your employer sends to you in January of each year that indicates how much you earned the year before and how much was deducted from your earnings to pay federal and state taxes.

> **ACTIVITY:** Have students circle the first instance of each word in the chapter.

BASIC FILING PROCEDURES

NOTE: This is an overview of each procedure. Each step is described in detail on the following pages.

Describe procedures

Your student activity text shows the basic steps you follow when you fill out your tax return form. Each step is explained in detail in the next pages.

1. **Add** up your total income: wages, salary, tips, interest.

2. **Subtract** your deductions: a standard amount or itemized.

3. **Subtract** your exemptions: an amount for you, your spouse, and each dependent.

Once you have subtracted the deductions and exemptions from your total income, you have your taxable income.

4. **Use** the tax tables to find how much tax you owe. Look up the taxable income in the tax tables. These tables are provided with the forms.

5. **Total** your credits and subtract them from the tax you owe. Credits include amounts allotted for child care and credit for elderly or disabled people. You may not be eligible for credits.

6. **Compare** the amount of tax you owe with the amount of tax withheld by your employer. You may receive a refund or you may owe more taxes.

CALCULATING YOUR INCOME

Describe Step 1

Add up all your wages, interest, and tips for the year.

Explain W-2 form

*   **Your employer must send you a W-2 form indicating how much income you earned for the year and the amount of taxes that were withheld.**

    If you worked for more than one employer, each employer must send you a W-2 form.

    If you worked as an independent contractor, you will receive a 1099 form and not a W-2 form.

    The employer must send you the form by January 31.

    A copy of the form also goes to the IRS.

Emphasize importance

If you don't receive the form, you should contact your employer. Be sure to keep the form in a safe place. It is a good idea to keep all tax-related papers and information in one place.

Explain 1099-INT form

- **Your bank must send you a 1099-INT form indicating how much interest income you earned for the year.**

  If you have more than one bank, each bank must send you a 1099-INT form.

  The bank must send you the form by January 31.

  A copy of the form also goes to the IRS.

Credit unions also use the 1099-INT. If you have other types of investments—for example, stocks—you may receive a 1099-DIV form. (DIV stands for "dividends.")

SAMPLE INCOME REPORT FORMS: W2 AND 1099-INT

Describe W-2 form

Your student activity text shows a blank example of the W-2 form that you will receive in the mail. The form you receive from your employers may look different, but each form has exactly the same sections.

ACTIVITY: W-2 Questions

1. Which section will show the amount of federal income tax withheld?
   Section 2

2. Which section will show the amount of state income tax withheld?
   Section 18

Describe 1099-INT form

Your student activity text shows a blank example of the 1099-INT form that you will receive in the mail. The form you receive from your bank may look different, but each form has exactly the same sections.

Some kinds of interest are not taxable. For example, interest on U.S. savings bonds sometimes is not taxed. However, it is shown on your 1099-INT.

ACTIVITY: 1099-INT Questions

1. Which section will show the amount of federal income tax withheld?
   Section 4

2. Which section will show the amount of interest income you earned that was not from U.S. savings bonds or Treasury bonds?   Section 1

SAMPLE INCOME REPORT FORMS: W-2

Describe forms

Your student activity text shows W-2 forms for two workers.

a Control number		
	OMB No. 1545-0008	

b Employer identification number 9511234567	1 Wages, tips, other compensation 15,000.00	2 Federal income tax withheld 1,638.00
c Employer's name, address, and ZIP code Quality Construction Labor Drive Impuesto, CA 90000	3 Social security wages 15,000.00	4 Social security tax withheld 930.00
	5 Medicare wages and tips 15,000.00	6 Medicare tax withheld 217.50
	7 Social security tips 0	8 Allocated tips
d Employee's social security number 123-45-6789	9 Advance EIC payment	10 Dependent care benefits
e Employee's name (first, middle initial, last) Joe Hernandez 300 Primavera Street APT A Impuesto, CA 90000	11 Nonqualified plans	12 Benefits included in box 1
	13 See instrs. for box 13	14 Other
f Employee's address and ZIP code	15 Statutory employee ☐ Deceased ☐ Pension plan ☐ Legal rep. ☐ Deferred compensation ☐	

16 State Employer's state I.D. no. CA	17 State wages, tips, etc. 15,000.00	18 State income tax 259.77	19 Locality name	20 Local wages, tips, etc. 15,000.00	21 Local income tax 195.09

a Control number		
	OMB No. 1545-0008	

b Employer identification number 9517654321	1 Wages, tips, other compensation 7,600.00	2 Federal income tax withheld 208.00
c Employer's name, address, and ZIP code Cathy's Cafe Main Street Midville, TX 70000	3 Social security wages 7,600.00	4 Social security tax withheld 4
	5 Medicare wages and tips 7,600.00	6 Medicare tax withheld 110.20
	7 Social security tips	8 Allocated tips
d Employee's social security number 987-65-4321	9 Advance EIC payment	10 Dependent care benefits
e Employee's name (first, middle initial, last) Kim Tranh 4300 Lakeview Avenue Midville, TX 70000	11 Nonqualified plans	12 Benefits included in box 1
	13 See instrs. for box 13	14 Other
f Employee's address and ZIP code	15 Statutory employee ☐ Deceased ☐ Pension plan ☐ Legal rep. ☐ Deferred compensation ☐	

16 State Employer's state I.D. no. TX	17 State wages, tips, etc. 7,600.00	18 State income tax 52.00	19 Locality name	20 Local wages, tips, etc. 7,600.00	21 Local income tax 48.80

W-2 FORM ACTIVITY

> **ACTIVITY:** Have students fill in the table (on page 32 of student activity text) using the sample W-2 forms and their own W-2 form if they have one. Review answers, then ask the questions that follow.

Ask questions

1. Look at sections 10, 12, 13, and 14 of the W-2 forms. Do you know why there are separate sections for Social Security and Medicare wages and tips?

   Income over a certain amount ($72,600 in 1998) is not taxed for Social Security. All wages are subject to Medicare tax.

2. What is Joe's Social Security number?

   123-45-6789

3. What is Kim's Social Security number?

   987-65-4321

DEDUCTIONS

Introduce Step 2

The second step in the basic filing procedure is to calculate your deductions and subtract them from your total income.

Define deduction

Deductions are subtracted, or deducted, from your total income to reduce your taxable income.

The effect of the deduction is to reduce the amount of income on which you must pay taxes.

Identify types

There are two basic kinds of deductions:

- **Standard deduction:** A fixed amount that is different for each filing status.

- **Itemized deductions:** A variable amount that you calculate according to IRS rules.

The two types are described in detail in the next sections.

STANDARD DEDUCTION

Review definition

The standard deduction is an amount that you can subtract from the income on which you are taxed.

Tax year 1998 standard deductions were:

- ☐ $4,250 for single people.
- ☐ $7,100 for married people filing jointly or for a widow(er) with a dependent child.
- ☐ $3,550 for a married person filing separately.
- ☐ $6,250 for a head of household.

NOTE: You may wish to point out deduction amounts for the current year.

Mention over 65 or blind

People who are 65 or older, or who are blind, receive a higher standard deduction.

Discuss nonresidents

If you are a nonresident of the United States, you cannot use the standard deduction unless you are married to a U.S. citizen.

> **ACTIVITY:** Ask students to place a check mark next to the standard deduction that applies to them.

Ask questions

1. If Joe Hernandez is single, what would be the amount of his standard deduction?

   $4,250

2. If Kim Tranh is married and has a child, what would be the amount of her standard deduction?

   $7,100

3. Mary Wong's husband died four years ago, and Mary has a six-year-old son. What would be the amount of her standard deduction?

   $6,250. For tax purposes, she is considered a head of household rather than a widow because her husband died more than two years ago.

ITEMIZED DEDUCTIONS

Describe itemizing

Some expenses that you have during the year can be deducted from your taxable income. These deductions are listed, or itemized, and you use this amount instead of the standard deduction.

Only expenses approved by the IRS can be deducted.

Mention long form

Some people should itemize their deductions. This means they must use the long form, Form 1040, for their tax return.

Describe when to itemize

You should itemize if your deductions add up to more than the standard deduction you are allowed.

Identify deductions

Deductions you can itemize include:

☐ Mortgage interest you paid on your home.

☐ A portion of medical and dental expenses you paid (not paid back to you by insurance).

☐ Taxes you paid (for example, state income tax and property taxes).

☐ Gifts to charity.

☐ Job expenses your employer did not pay for (such as union dues).

Discuss records

You must keep very good records if you itemize your deductions.

Emphasize rules

You must be very careful to follow the IRS rules about what is a deduction and what is not.

Describe when to use standard deduction

Use the standard deduction if it is more than the total of the itemized deductions you can claim.

Ask questions

1. Steve Carlson is married and has mortgage interest of $5,000. He paid $4,000 in state and property taxes and contributed $400 to charity. Should he itemize or use the standard deduction?

   He should itemize. He has $9,400 in deductions, and the standard deduction is only $7,100 for married people.

2. Marcia Edelman is single. She paid $3,200 in rent for the year. She paid $2,900 in state taxes and contributed $100 to charity. Should she itemize or use the standard deduction?

   She should use the standard deduction. She has only $3,000 in deductions, and the standard deduction for single people is $4,250. Rent is not deductible.

IRA DEDUCTIONS

Introduce IRA

There is another kind of deduction you may be able to take in addition to the standard or itemized deductions:

- IRA (individual retirement arrangement)

Describe IRAs

Persons who have taxable income for the year may be able to deduct up to $2,000 in a special IRA savings account. This depends on certain conditions, such as income level and whether the person has a retirement plan at work.

- You deduct the money you put in this account from your total income. Therefore, the IRA money is not taxed this year.

- You can't use the money in the IRA account until you are $59\frac{1}{2}$ years old. If you withdraw it sooner, you must pay taxes and penalties.

NOTE: Contributions to IRAs may be in stocks, mutual funds, money market funds, and many other kinds of investments in addition to savings accounts. The account must be designated as an IRA by completing the appropriate paperwork.

IRA funds are taxed when they are withdrawn after retirement. IRAs are a means of deferring taxes. Presumably, retired taxpayers will be taxed at a lower rate than when they were working.

EXEMPTIONS

Introduce Step 3

Exemptions are subtracted from your total income to reduce your taxable income.

NOTE: You may wish to provide the current exemption amounts if they have changed.

Identify types

There are two types of exemptions: personal and dependent.

Personal exemptions

- You are allowed one personal exemption for yourself and one for your spouse.

- Each personal exemption reduces your taxable income by $2,700.

Dependent exemptions

- You are allowed one exemption for each dependent you claim on your form.

- Each dependent exemption reduces your taxable income by $2,700.

- Each dependent must meet the five specified requirements to qualify for the exemption.

- The requirements for a dependent are given in Chapter 4.

Ask questions

1. Steve Carlson is married and has one six-year-old son. How many exemptions may he claim on his tax form? What is the total dollar amount of exemptions?

   Three; $8,100

2. Marcia Edelman is single and has no children. How many exemptions may she claim on her tax for? What is the total dollar amount of exemptions?

   One; $2,700

TAX TABLES

Review steps

The first three steps in the basic filing procedures are to:

1. Add up your total income.

2. Subtract your deductions.

3. Subtract your exemptions.

Once you have done this, you have calculated your taxable income.

Introduce Step 4

Once you have figured your taxable income, you can use the tax tables to find the amount of tax you owe.

- Tax tables are provided with the forms.

- You must know your filing status to figure your tax, because the tax tables have separate columns for each filing status.

- You look up the amount of taxable income, not the total income.

Discuss tax table

Your student activity text shows a section of a tax table. Look at the columns for each different filing status. On the left is the amount of taxable income. In the columns on the right are the amounts of tax owed for each amount of income and each filing status.

Refer to back of book

In the back of your student activity text is a complete set of tax tables. Please take a brief look at them now.

Sample tax table

If line 39 (taxable income) is—		And you are—			
At least	But less than	Single	Married filing jointly	Married filing separately	Head of a household
		Your tax is—			
17,000					
17,000	17,050	2,554	2,554	2,554	2,554
17,050	17,100	2,561	2,561	2,561	2,561
17,100	17,150	2,569	2,569	2,569	2,569
17,150	17,200	2,576	2,576	2,576	2,576
17,200	17,250	2,584	2,584	2,584	2,584
17,250	17,300	2,591	2,591	2,591	2,591
17,300	17,350	2,599	2,599	2,599	2,599
17,350	17,400	2,606	2,606	2,606	2,606
17,400	17,450	2,614	2,614	2,614	2,614
17,450	17,500	2,621	2,621	2,621	2,621
17,500	17,550	2,629	2,629	2,629	2,629
17,550	17,600	2,636	2,636	2,636	2,636
17,600	17,650	2,644	2,644	2,644	2,644
17,650	17,700	2,651	2,651	2,651	2,651
17,700	17,750	2,659	2,659	2,659	2,659
17,750	17,800	2,666	2,666	2,666	2,666
17,800	17,850	2,674	2,674	2,674	2,674
17,850	17,900	2,681	2,681	2,681	2,681
17,900	17,950	2,689	2,689	2,689	2,689
17,950	18,000	2,696	2,696	2,696	2,696
18,000					
18,000	18,050	2,704	2,704	2,704	2,704
18,050	18,100	2,711	2,711	2,711	2,711
18,100	18,150	2,719	2,719	2,719	2,719
18,150	18,200	2,726	2,726	2,726	2,726
18,200	18,250	2,734	2,734	2,734	2,734
18,250	18,300	2,741	2,741	2,741	2,741
18,300	18,350	2,749	2,749	2,749	2,749
18,350	18,400	2,756	2,756	2,756	2,756
18,400	18,450	2,764	2,764	2,764	2,764
18,450	18,500	2,771	2,771	2,771	2,771
18,500	18,550	2,779	2,779	2,779	2,779
18,550	18,600	2,786	2,786	2,786	2,786
18,600	18,650	2,794	2,794	2,794	2,794

TAX TABLE EXERCISE

ACTIVITY: Have students complete the tax table exercise.

Mary Wong is single. She has one six-year-old child. She calculated her taxable income as $17,942 for 1998.

NOTE: Answers are included in what follows for your convenience.

1. What is her filing status?

   Head of household

2. Refer to the tax table to determine how much her tax is. Write the amount here:

   $2,689

TAX CREDITS

Introduce Step 5

A tax credit is an amount you can subtract from the amount of taxes you owe. Two examples of tax credits are described here.

Child and dependent care credit

You can receive a credit of up to 30% of your expenses if you pay someone to care for:

- Your dependent under age 13.
- Your disabled spouse or other dependent.

You can get this credit if you are working. If you are looking for work, you may also receive this credit, but you must have an income during the year.

Credit for the elderly or the disabled

A credit is available for persons within certain income limits who are:

- 65 or older.
- Under 65 but retired on permanent and total disability and had taxable disability income.

Discuss no credits

If you do not have any credits, do not subtract anything from the amount you owe.

Introduce Step 6

Once you have calculated the amount of taxes you owe, you must compare this amount with the amount that was withheld from your paychecks.

- If you owe less than what was withheld from the paycheck, you will receive a refund when you file your tax return.
- If you owe more than what was withheld from your paycheck, you owe taxes and must send money to the IRS when you file your tax return.

NOTE: The next exercise includes this step.

BASIC TAX CALCULATION EXERCISE

ACTIVITY: Have students complete the tax calculation exercise using the tax tables at the back of their books.

NOTE: Answers are supplied here for your convenience.

Joe Hernandez is single and has no dependents. He earned $15,000 from one job and $3,500 from another job. His savings account at the bank earned $200 in interest. He has about $1,000 in deductions. He had $2,013 withheld from his pay. Please calculate the following:

1. **Total income** $18,700

   (Wages + interest)

2. **Deductions** $14,250

   (Write the larger of standard or itemized deductions.)

3. **Exemptions** $2,700

   (Number of exemptions × $2,700)

   Taxable income $11,750

(Subtract lines 2 and 3 from line 1.)

4. **Taxes owed** $11,766

   (Refer to the tax tables. Look up the taxable income under the correct column for Joe's filing status. Write the amount of taxes he owes.)

5. **Joe is not eligible for any credits, so nothing is subtracted from the taxes owed.**

6. **Will he receive a refund, or does he have to pay more taxes?**

   (Compare the amount in line 4 with the amount withheld.)

Amount withheld	Refund
☐ How much?	$ 247

NOTE: Subtract the taxes owed ($1,766) from the amount withheld ($2,013) to determine the amount of the refund.

WHAT FORM DO YOU NEED?

Introduce forms

There are different kinds of tax return forms for different situations.

NOTE: Form requirements are valid for the 1998 tax year.

Short forms

☐ **1040-EZ**

- Very short.
- Uses the standard deduction.
- "Single" or "married filing jointly" filing status only.
- For very simple tax situations.

☐ **1040A**

- Short.
- Uses the standard deduction.
- For any filing status.
- For simple tax situations.

Long form

☐ **1040**

- Long.
- May itemize deductions or use standard deduction.
- For any filing status.
- For more complex tax situations.

> **ACTIVITY:** Have students place a check mark next to the type of form they think they need.

NOTE: The next two chapters provide practice with the 1040EZ and the 1040A. The 1040 covers so many different kinds of situations and deductions that it is beyond the scope of a classroom exercise.

WHERE DO YOU GET THE FORMS?

Identify access to forms

There are many ways to obtain the forms.

- **Mail**

  If you filed last year and live at the same address, you will receive forms in the mail.

- **Post office**

- **Public library**

  At some libraries, you have to pay to make photocopies of the library's forms.

- **Bank**
- **Local IRS office**
- **Telephone:** 1-800-829-3676 (1-800-TAX-FORM)
- **The Internet:** www.irs.ustreas.gov

ACTIVITY: For homework, have students obtain the type of form they think they will need.

NOTE: It may be difficult to get forms from non-IRS locations once tax season is over. However, the IRS may be able to provide forms.

SUMMARY OF INFORMATION

List information needed

The following is a summary of information you need before you begin to fill out your tax return forms.

- Social Security numbers for you, your spouse, and your dependents one year old or older.
- W-2 form(s) from your employer(s).
- 1099-MISC forms if you were self-employed.
- 1099-INT form(s) from your bank(s).
- Receipts and records of deductions if you plan to itemize.

Mention record keeping

Remember to keep all your tax-related papers and information together in the same place so you can find these materials when necessary. It is also a good idea to keep the stubs from your paychecks to verify that the W-2 forms are correct.

It is generally recommended that you keep all your tax records for five to seven years in case you are audited by the IRS.

REVIEW OF FILING PROCEDURES

Review procedures

The basic filing procedures are:

1. **Add** up your total income.
2. **Subtract** your deductions.
3. **Subtract** your exemptions.

Once you have subtracted the deductions and exemptions from your total income, you have your **taxable income**.

4. **Use** the tax tables to find out how much tax you owe.
5. **Total** your credits and subtract them from the tax you owe.
6. **Compare** the tax you owe with the tax withheld from your paycheck to determine if you receive a refund or if you owe more taxes.

CHAPTER 6

Filling Out Forms—1040EZ

OVERVIEW

Topics

- Filling out the 1040EZ

Objectives

By the end of this chapter, the students will be able to:

- Fill out the 1040EZ tax return form.

Student activities

- Complete the 1040EZ.

Things you need

- You may wish to distribute enough 1040EZ forms so that students can work with them separately from the student activity text. It will be easier to work with the form this way.

- If you will have students complete tax forms using their own information, they will need their tax information (see end of Chapter 5).

- Publication 17 will be useful for answering questions.

Important points

- The exercises in this chapter are based on 1998 information. This was the latest information available when the manuscript was completed. Be sure students understand this.

- If none of your students will use the 1040EZ, you may skip this chapter and go on to Chapter 7, which discusses the 1040A. However, since the 1040EZ is simpler, it can be a good introduction to working with forms.

- At the end of the exercise, you may wish to have participants repeat the exercise using tax forms for the current year. You will need to create your own answer key.

- If you have participants complete the forms with their own tax information, you should use current forms, if available. Contact the IRS to inquire if a volunteer from VITA is available to assist you during this activity.

- Most people consider their financial situation highly personal. If students do not wish to reveal their own information, we recommend that you respect their wishes.

FILLING OUT FORMS— 1040EZ

Describe chapter

In this chapter, you will learn about:

- Filling out the 1040EZ form.
  We will go step by step through the form so that you understand each section.

Before we go any further, let's discuss the vocabulary for this chapter.

VOCABULARY

ACTIVITY: Before providing the definitions, ask for volunteers to define each word. Write brief definitions on a transparency or on the board, or send volunteers to the board to record their definitions. Have the class refine the sentence structure and spelling of each.

Have the students use each word in a sentence.

sighted: Not blind.

taxable income: Income upon which you must pay taxes. Not all income is taxed.

claim: To list. For example, you must list, or claim, the deductions and exemptions on your income tax forms.

dividends: Money you receive from stocks or investments. Dividends are generally a type of taxable income.

tax-exempt: Not taxable. Some type of interest and dividends are not considered taxable, usually because they are received from public agencies.

ACTIVITY: Have students circle the first instance of each word in the chapter.

INSTRUCTIONS

Discuss instructions

- Read the information about Joe Hernandez, the sample taxpayer.
- Read the explanation of the 1040EZ form in this chapter.
- Complete the form using the information about the sample taxpayer.

NOTE: You can conduct this exercise in several ways.

For example, you may have students read the scenario about Joe Hernandez and fill out the form as you review each section.

Alternatively, you may have students read the scenario, then review each section so that they understand it, and then complete the form at the end.

1040EZ PRACTICE EXERCISE

ACTIVITY: Have students fill out the 1040EZ form for Joe Hernandez.

Joe Hernandez

Joe Hernandez is a carpenter. He is single and has no dependents.

He earned $15,000 from one job and later earned $3,500 from another job.

His savings account at the bank earned $200 in interest. He has about $1,000 in deductions.

He had a total of $2,013 withheld from his pay.

He lives at 300 Primavera Street, Apt. A, Impuesto, CA 90000. His Social Security number is 123-45-6789, and he would like to contribute to the Presidential Election Campaign fund.

WHO CAN USE THE 1040EZ?

Identify requirements

You can use the 1040EZ if you meet the following requirements:

- Sighted single person under 65.
- Sighted married couple under 65 filing jointly.
- Total taxable income of $50,000 or less.
- Taxable interest income of $400 or less.
- No dependents.
- U.S. resident.
- Uses standard deduction. May NOT itemize deductions.
- All taxable income comes from earnings reported on W-2 and interest (no rental income or income from own business).

> **ACTIVITY:** Can Joe Hernandez use the 1040EZ? Why or why not?
>
> Yes. He is single with no dependents. His income is lower than the required limits. He only has about $1,000 in deductions, so he prefers to use the standard deduction. He lives in California, so he is a U.S. resident.

Ask questions

1. Steve Carlson is married and has one dependent child. He has mortgage interest of $5,000. He paid $4,000 in state taxes and contributed $400 to charity. Can he use the 1040EZ? Why or why not?

   No. He has a dependent. Also, he should itemize rather than use the standard deduction.

2. Bob Deauville is a 17-year-old unmarried high school student in Maine. He works at a fast-food restaurant and earned $4,600. He has no dependents. Can he use the 1040EZ? Why or why not?

   Yes. He is single with no dependents. His income is lower than the required limits. He won't have many deductions, so he will not itemize deductions. He lives in Maine, so he is a resident of the United States.

> **ACTIVITY:** If you want students to determine if they can use the 1040EZ, have them place a check in each box that applies to their situation. If they check all the boxes, they can use the 1040EZ.

Point out form

The student activity text contains a blank copy of both sides of the one-page 1040EZ form.

NOTE: The form is for the 1998 tax year.

1040EZ—SIDE 1

Department of the Treasury—Internal Revenue Service

Form
1040EZ

**Income Tax Return for Single and
Joint Filers With No Dependents** (99) **1998**   OMB No. 1545-0675

Use
the
IRS
label
here

Your first name and initial   Last name

If a joint return, spouse's first name and initial   Last name

Home address (number and street). If you have a P.O. box, see page 7.   Apt. no.

City, town or post office, state, and ZIP code. If you have a foreign address, see page 7.

Your social security number

Spouse s social security number

▲ **IMPORTANT!** ▲
You **must** enter
your SSN(s) above.

**Presidential
Election
Campaign**
(See page 7.)

Note: *Checking Yes will not change your tax or reduce your refund.*

Do you want $3 to go to this fund?   ▶ Yes ☐ No ☐

If a joint return, does your spouse want $3 to go to this fund?   ▶ Yes ☐ No ☐

Income

**Attach
Copy B of
Form(s)
W-2 here.**
Enclose, but
do not staple,
any payment.

Note: *You
must check
Yes or No.*

1 Total wages, salaries, and tips. This
should be shown in box 1 of your
W-2 form(s). Attach your W-2 form(s).   1

2 Taxable interest income. If the total is over $400, you
cannot use Form 1040EZ.   2

3 Unemployment compensation (see page 8).   3

4 Add lines 1, 2, and 3. This is your **adjusted gross
income.** If under $10,030, see page 9 to find out if you
can claim the earned income credit on line 8a.   4

5 Can your parents (or someone else) claim you on their return?
Yes. Enter amount   **No.** If **single,** enter 6,950.00.
from worksheet   If **married,** enter 12,500.00.
☐ on back.   ☐ See back for explanation.   5

6 Subtract line 5 from line 4. If line 5 is larger than
line 4, enter 0. This is your **taxable income.**   ▶ 6

Dollars   Cents

**Payments
and tax**

7 Enter your Federal income tax withheld from box 2 of
your W-2 form(s).   7

8a **Earned income credit** (see page 9).
b Nontaxable earned income: enter type and amount below.

Type $ 8a

9 Add lines 7 and 8a. These are your **total payments.**   9

10 **Tax.** Use the amount on **line 6 above** to find your tax
in the tax table on pages 20—24 of the booklet. Then,
enter the tax from the table on this line.   10

Refund

Have it
directly
deposited! See
page 12 and
fill in 11b,
11c, and 11d.

11a If line 9 is larger than line 10, subtract line 10 from
line 9. This is your **refund.**   11a

▶ **b** Routing number

▶ **c** Type: Checking   Savings   **d** Account
number
☐   ☐   ↳

**Amount
you owe**

12 If line 10 is larger than line 9, subtract line 9 from line
10. This is the **amount you owe.** See page 14 for
details on how to pay.   12

I have read this return. Under penalties of perjury, I declare that to the best of my knowledge and belief, the
return is true, correct, and accurately lists all amounts and sources of income I received during the tax year.

**Sign
here** ▶

Keep copy for
your records.

Your signature   Spouse s signature if joint return. See page 7.

Date   Your occupation   Date   Spouse s occupation

For
Official
Use
Only

1 2 3 4 5

6 7 8 9 10

For Disclosure, Privacy Act, and Paperwork Reduction Act Notice, see page 18.   Cat. No. 11329W   **1998 Form 1040EZ**

Form **1040EZ**

Department of the Treasury—Internal Revenue Service

Income Tax Return for Single and Joint Filers With No Dependents (99) **1998**

OMB No. 1545-0675

Use the IRS label here

Your first name and initial: **Joe** Last name: **Hernandez**

If a joint return, spouse's first name and initial Last name

Home address (number and street). If you have a P.O. box, see page 7. **300 Primavera St.** Apt. no. **A**

City, town or post office, state, and ZIP code. If you have a foreign address, see page 7. **Impuesto, CA 90000**

Your social security number 1 2 3 | 4 5 | 6 7 8 9

Spouse s social security number

▲ **IMPORTANT!** ▲
You **must** enter your SSN(s) above.

Presidential Election Campaign (See page 7.)

Note: *Checking Yes will not change your tax or reduce your refund.*

Do you want $3 to go to this fund? ▶ Yes ☑ No ☐

If a joint return, does your spouse want $3 to go to this fund? ▶ Yes ☐ No ☐

		Dollars	Cents

Income

Attach Copy B of Form(s) W-2 here. Enclose, but do not staple, any payment.

1 Total wages, salaries, and tips. This should be shown in box 1 of your W-2 form(s). Attach your W-2 form(s). — 1 — **18,500.00**

2 Taxable interest income. If the total is over $400, you cannot use Form 1040EZ. — 2 — **200.00**

3 Unemployment compensation (see page 8). — 3 — **0.00**

4 Add lines 1, 2, and 3. This is your **adjusted gross income.** If under $10,030, see page 9 to find out if you can claim the earned income credit on line 8a. — 4 — **18,700.00**

Note: *You must check Yes or No.*

5 Can your parents (or someone else) claim you on their return?
Yes. Enter amount from worksheet on back. ☐
No. ☑ If **single,** enter 6,950.00. If **married,** enter 12,500.00. See back for explanation. — 5 — **6,950.00**

6 Subtract line 5 from line 4. If line 5 is larger than line 4, enter 0. This is your **taxable income.** ▶ 6 — **11,750.00**

Payments and tax

7 Enter your Federal income tax withheld from box 2 of your W-2 form(s). — 7 — **2,013.00**

8a Earned income credit (see page 9).
b Nontaxable earned income: enter type and amount below.
Type _____ $ _____ — 8a — **0.00**

9 Add lines 7 and 8a. These are your **total payments.** — 9 — **2,013.00**

10 Tax. Use the amount on **line 6 above** to find your tax in the tax table on pages 20—24 of the booklet. Then, enter the tax from the table on this line. — 10 — **1,766.00**

Refund

Have it directly deposited! See page 12 and fill in 11b, 11c, and 11d.

11a If line 9 is larger than line 10, subtract line 10 from line 9. This is your **refund.** — 11a — **247.00**

b Routing number
c Type: ☐ Checking ☐ Savings **d** Account number

Amount you owe

12 If line 10 is larger than line 9, subtract line 9 from line 10. This is the **amount you owe.** See page 14 for details on how to pay. — 12 —

I have read this return. Under penalties of perjury, I declare that to the best of my knowledge and belief, the return is true, correct, and accurately lists all amounts and sources of income I received during the tax year.

Sign here

Keep copy for your records.

Your signature Date
Spouse s signature if joint return. See page 7. Date

Your occupation: **carpenter** Spouse s occupation

For Official Use Only
1 2 3 4 5
6 7 8 9 10

For Disclosure, Privacy Act, and Paperwork Reduction Act Notice, see page 18.

Cat. No. 11329W **1998 Form 1040EZ**

1040EZ—SIDE 2

1998 Form 1040EZ page 2

Use this form if	• Your filing status is single or married filing jointly. • You (and your spouse if married) were under 65 on January 1, 1999, and not blind at the end of 1998.

Use this form if

• Your filing status is single or married filing jointly.

• You (and your spouse if married) were under 65 on January 1, 1999, and not blind at the end of 1998.

• You do not claim any dependents.

• Your taxable income (line 6) is less than $50,000.

• You do not claim a student loan interest deduction or an education credit. See page 3.

• You had only wages, salaries, tips, taxable scholarship or fellowship grants, unemployment compensation, or Alaska Permanent Fund dividends, and your taxable interest income was not over $400. But if you earned tips, including allocated tips, that are not included in box 5 and box 7 of your W-2, you may not be able to use Form 1040EZ. See page 8.

• You did not receive any advance earned income credit payments.

If you are not sure about your filing status, see page 7. If you have questions about dependents, use TeleTax topic 354 (see page 17). If you cannot use this form, use TeleTax topic 352 (see page 17).

Filling in your return

For tips on how to avoid common mistakes, see page 25.

Enter your (and your spouse's if married) social security number on the front. Because this form is read by a machine, please print your numbers inside the boxes like this:

9 8 7 6 5 4 3 2 1 0   Do not type your numbers. Do not use dollar signs.

If you received a scholarship or fellowship grant or tax-exempt interest income, such as on municipal bonds, see the booklet before filling in the form. Also, see the booklet if you received a Form 1099-INT showing Federal income tax withheld or if Federal income tax was withheld from your unemployment compensation or Alaska Permanent Fund dividends.

Remember, you must report all wages, salaries, and tips even if you do not get a W-2 form from your employer. You must also report all your taxable interest income, including interest from banks, savings and loans, credit unions, etc., even if you do not get a Form 1099-INT.

Worksheet for dependents who checked "Yes" on line 5

Use this worksheet to figure the amount to enter on line 5 if someone can claim you (or your spouse if married) as a dependent, even if that person chooses not to do so. To find out if someone can claim you as a dependent, use TeleTax topic 354 (see page 17).

A. Amount, if any, from line 1 on front _____

  + _____250.00_ Enter total ▶ A. _____

B. Minimum standard deduction . . . . B. _____700.00

C. Enter the LARGER of line A or line B here . . . . C. _____

D. Maximum standard deduction. If single, enter 4,250.00; if married, enter 7,100.00 . . . . D. _____

E. Enter the SMALLER of line C or line D here. This is your standard deduction . . . . E. _____

F. Exemption amount.
  • If single, enter 0.
  • If married and—
    —both you and your spouse can be claimed as dependents, enter 0.
    —only one of you can be claimed as a dependent, enter 2,700.00. } F. _____

G. Add lines E and F. Enter the total here and on line 5 on the front . . G. _____

If you checked "No" on line 5 because no one can claim you (or your spouse if married) as a dependent, enter on line 5 the amount shown below that applies to you.

• Single, enter 6,950.00. This is the total of your standard deduction (4,250.00) and your exemption (2,700.00).

• Married, enter 12,500.00. This is the total of your standard deduction (7,100.00), your exemption (2,700.00), and your spouse's exemption (2,700.00).

Mailing return

Mail your return by   April 15, 1999.   Use the envelope that came with your booklet. If you do not have that envelope, see page 28 for the address to use.

Paid preparer's use only

See page 14.

Under penalties of perjury, I declare that I have examined this return, and to the best of my knowledge and belief, it is true, correct, and accurately lists all amounts and sources of income received during the tax year. This declaration is based on all information of which I have any knowledge.

Preparer's signature ▶	Date	Check if self-employed ☐	Preparer's SSN

Firm's name (or yours if self-employed) and address ▶	EIN
	ZIP code

SECTION 1: NAME AND ADDRESS

Refer to blank 1040EZ

Your student activity text contains a blank sample of 1040EZ.

	Department of the Treasury—Internal Revenue Service	
Form **1040EZ**	**Income Tax Return for Single and Joint Filers With No Dependents** (99) **1998**	OMB No. 1545-0675

Use the IRS label here

Your first name and initial	Last name
If a joint return, spouse's first name and initial	Last name
Home address (number and street). If you have a P.O. box, see page 7.	Apt. no.
City, town or post office, state, and ZIP code. If you have a foreign address, see page 7.	

Your social security number

Spouse's social security number

▲ **IMPORTANT!** ▲
You **must** enter your SSN(s) above.

Presidential Election Campaign
(See page 7.)

Note: *Checking "Yes" will not change your tax or reduce your refund.*
Do you want $3 to go to this fund? ► Yes ☐ No ☐
If a joint return, does your spouse want $3 to go to this fund? ► Yes ☐ No ☐

Describe Section 1

In the initial section of the 1040EZ form, you print personal information.

Name, address, and Social Security number

- **In the large rectangle, print your and your spouse's:**
  First name, initial, and last (family) name.
  Home address: number, street, and apartment number.
  City, state, and ZIP code.

- **In the boxes to the right of the large rectangle, print your and your spouse's Social Security numbers.**

NOTE: If students are originally from other countries, it is important that they understand the appropriate way to complete the form. Names and addresses are written differently in other countries.

Presidential Election Campaign contribution

In this section, you must decide whether you want the IRS to contribute $3.00 of your tax money to a special fund to help pay for presidential election costs.

This will not increase your tax owed or decrease the amount of your refund. The money the IRS contributes to this fund is money that you have already paid.

- Mark an X in the first Yes box if you do want the IRS to contribute $3.00 to the special fund. Or mark an X in the first No box if you do *not* want the IRS to contribute $3.00 to the special fund.

- Mark an X in the second Yes box if your spouse does want the IRS to contribute $3.00 to the special fund. Or mark an X in the second No box if your spouse does *not* want the IRS to contribute $3.00 to the special fund.

SECTION 2: REPORTING YOUR INCOME

Describe Section 2

In this section of the 1040EZ, you print financial information. You must also indicate whether your parents (or anyone else) can claim you as a dependent on their income tax return.

1. Add up wages, salaries, and tips. Print the total in the boxes to the right of 1.

   - Add up the amounts on your W-2 form(s).

   - You will have to attach your W-2 form(s) when you have completed the 1040EZ.

2. Add up total interest income. Print the total in the boxes to the right of 2.

   - Add up the amounts from your 1099-INT form(s).

   - The amount must be $400 or less.

3. Add up unemployment compensation. Print the total in the boxes to the right of 3.

4. Add lines 1, 2, and 3. Print this total in the boxes to the right of 4.

5. Mark an X:

   • In the Yes box if your parents or someone else can claim you as a dependent on their income tax report.

   If you mark the Yes box, you must complete the Standard Deduction worksheet that follows and print the amount from line G in the boxes on the right.

   • In the No box if no one claims you as a dependent on their income tax report.

   If you mark the No box in the boxes to the right of 5, print $6,950 if you are single or $12,500 if you are married filing jointly. This is the total of your standard deduction (either $4,250 or $7,100) and your personal exemption(s) ($2,700 for each person).

NOTE: If your students are claimed as dependents, you may go on to the next topic and then return to Step 6 on this page.

---

6. Subtract the amount on line 5 from the amount on line 4 (only if the amount on line 4 is larger than the amount on line 5).

   • Print the remainder in the boxes to the right of 6.

   • If 5 is larger than 4, print 0 (zero) in the boxes to the right of 6.

   • This amount is your taxable income.

STANDARD DEDUCTION WORKSHEET

Describe when to use worksheet

This worksheet is only for those who marked an X in the Yes box in 5. This means that the taxpayer or the taxpayer's spouse can be claimed as a dependent of someone else, often a parent.

You can find the worksheet on the back of form 1040EZ. If you marked No in 5, go to Section 3, "Figuring Your Tax."

NOTE: You can skip this section if all students marked No.

Worksheet for dependents who checked "Yes" on line 5

Use this worksheet to figure the amount to enter on line 5 if someone can claim you (or your spouse if married) as a dependent, even if that person chooses not to do so. To find out if someone can claim you as a dependent, use TeleTax topic 354 (see page 17).

A. Amount, if any, from line 1 on front _____

    + _____250.00_____ Enter total ▶ A. _____

B. Minimum standard deduction . . . . B. _____700.00_____

C. Enter the LARGER of line A or line B here . . . . C. _____

D. Maximum standard deduction. If single, enter 4,250.00; if married, enter 7,100.00 . . . . D. _____

E. Enter the SMALLER of line C or line D here. This is your standard deduction . . . . E. _____

F. Exemption amount.
   • If single, enter 0.
   • If married and
       both you and your spouse can be claimed as dependents, enter 0.
       only one of you can be claimed as a dependent, enter 2,700.00.   F. _____

G. Add lines E and F. Enter the total here and on line 5 on the front . . G. _____

If you checked No on line 5   because no one can claim you (or your spouse if married) as a dependent, enter on line 5 the amount shown below that applies to you.

• Single, enter 6,950.00. This is the total of your standard deduction (4,250.00) and your exemption (2,700.00).

• Married, enter 12,500.00. This is the total of your standard deduction (7,100.00), your exemption (2,700.00), and your spouse s exemption (2,700.00).

Describe worksheet

Here's how to complete the worksheet.

- **On line A, add the amount from line 1 to $250.00.**

- **On line C, print the larger number:**

  Either the total income (line A)

  OR

  $700.00 (line B).

- **On line D, print $4,250.00 if you are single or $7,100.00 if you are married filing jointly.**

- **On line E, print the smaller number:**

  Either the amount on line C

  OR

  The amount on line D.

- **On line F, print the exemption amount ($0 or $2,700.00).**

- **On line G, add the amounts on lines E and F.**

- **Write the line G number on line 5 on the 1040EZ.**

  This gives you the amount of the deduction you can take.

NOTE: The result of this calculation is that the taxpayer may take up to the full standard deduction but will not get the personal exemption of $2,700 that a nondependent can claim. In some cases, usually for part-time workers, the deduction will be less than the standard. If the individual earned only $2,500, for example, this will be their deduction, rather than $4,250.

ACTIVITY: If you have students who can be claimed as dependents and who can use the 1040EZ, practice using this worksheet with different amount of total income.

NOTE: You may need to go back to the previous section ("Reporting your income") so that students can complete line 6.

SECTION 3: FIGURING YOUR TAX

Describe figuring tax

In this section of the 1040EZ, you figure the amount of income tax already withheld from paychecks. Then you look in the tax tables to find out how much tax is owed.

Payments and tax

7 Enter your Federal income tax withheld from box 2 of your W-2 form(s).   7

8a **Earned income credit** (see page 9).

   b Nontaxable earned income: enter type and amount below.

Type	$

    8a

9 Add lines 7 and 8a. These are your **total payments.**   9

10 **Tax.** Use the amount on **line 6 above** to find your tax in the tax table on pages 20–24 of the booklet. Then, enter the tax from the table on this line.   10

7. Look at box 2 of the W-2 form to find the total federal income tax withheld. If you have more than one W-2 form, add the amounts from each one.

   • Print the total federal income tax withheld in the boxes to the right of 7.

8. If your (and your spouse's) income is less than $10,030, you may be eligible to receive a special credit—called the earned income credit.

   To receive this credit, you must fulfill the following four requirements:

   • you (and your spouse) must be at least 25 years old, but under the age of 65 in 1998

   • you (and your spouse) cannot be claimed as a dependent on someone else's 1998 income tax (see 5 earlier)

   • you (and your spouse) must have lived in the United States for more than six months in 1998

- you (can your spouse) received less than $10,030 of taxable and nontaxable earned income in 1998

8a. If you fulfill these four requirements, print EIC in the space to the right of the word "below" on line 8b. The IRS will calculate this credit for you.

8b. Certain types of income are not taxable but you must include them on your 1040EZ to see if you qualify to receive the earned income tax credit. Examples of nontaxable earned income are housing allowances or meals and lodging provided by your employer or the military.

NOTE: Welfare, SSI, and Food Stamps are NOT earned income. Do not include them in 8b.

If you received nontaxable earned income, write the type and the amount on 8b.

If you are eligible for the earned income credit, leave the rest of the 1040EZ blank, except for your (and your spouse's) signature.

If you are NOT eligible for the earned income credit, write 0 in the boxes to the right of 8a and continue to complete this form, lines 9 to 12.

9.   Add the amounts on line 7 and line 8a. These are your **total payments.**

10.   Look in the tax tables and find the taxable income you wrote on line 6. Then find in the tax table how much you owe on the line 6 amount.

- Print the amount of your tax in the boxes to the right of 10.

NOTE: Tax tables are included at the back of the student activity text and at the end of this teacher's guide. Each year, the tables are updated and included with the instructions for each annually revised form.

If students need a refresher on using the tax tables, refer back to Chapter 5, "Tax tables" and "Tax table exercise."

SECTION 4: REFUND OR TAXES OWED

Describe comparing amounts

In this section of the 1040EZ, you must compare the amount of money withheld from paychecks with the amount of taxes listed in the tax tables.

Refund

Have it directly deposited! See page 12 and fill in 11b, 11c, and 11d.

11a If line 9 is larger than line 10, subtract line 10 from line 9. This is your **refund.**

11a ☐ , ☐☐☐ . ☐☐

▶ **b** Routing number

▶ **c** Type:
    Checking   Savings
    ☐   ☐

d Account number

Amount you owe

12 If line 10 is larger than line 9, subtract line 9 from line 10. This is the **amount you owe.** See page 14 for details on how to pay.

12 ☐ , ☐☐☐ . ☐☐

11a. Look at the amount on line 9. If it is larger than the amount on line 10, subtract 10 from 9 (line 9 − line 10).

- Print the result in the boxes to the right of 11a.

- You have paid too much in taxes and you will receive a refund.

- The IRS will now directly deposit your refund in the bank if you have a checking or savings account. This is a good idea because it prevents lost or stolen income tax refund checks. If you prefer to receive a refund check, leave 11b, 11c, and 11d blank.

11b. Print the routing number of your bank. (Ask the bank for this nine-digit number.)

11c. Put an X in the correct box to indicate whether your income tax refund is to be deposited into your checking or savings account.

11d. Write your account number in the boxes.

12. If the amount on line 9 is smaller than the amount on line 10, then subtract 9 from 10 (line 10 − line 9).

- Print the result in the boxes to the right of 12. (Line 11a will remain blank.)

- You owe this amount of taxes to the IRS.

- Prepare a check or money order payable to the IRS for this amount.

- Print your name, address, Social Security number, daytime telephone number, and "Year_ Form 1040EZ" on the check or money order.

NOTE: Year_ is used to indicate that the students should write the current tax year on their checks. For example, if they are filing on April 15, 1999, they would write "1998 Form 1040EZ" on their check or money order.

SECTION 5: SIGNATURE

Describe signing the form

In this final section of the 1040EZ, you must sign and date your income tax report.

I have read this return. Under penalties of perjury, I declare that to the best of my knowledge and belief, the return is true, correct, and accurately lists all amounts and sources of income I received during the tax year.

Sign here ▶

Keep copy for your records.

Your signature	Spouse s signature if joint return. See page 7.
Date	Your occupation	Date	Spouse s occupation

For Official Use Only

1 2 3 4 5
6 7 8 9 10

For Disclosure, Privacy Act, and Paperwork Reduction Act Notice, see page 18.   Cat. No. 11329W   **1998 Form 1040EZ**

- Sign your name. If you are married, your spouse also needs to sign, date, and write his or her occupation.
- Print the date on the line below your signature.
- Beside the date, write what your occupation is.

1040EZ FINAL PROCEDURES

Identify final steps
- Make a copy of the tax return for your records.
- Staple Copy B of your W-2 form(s) to the original 1040EZ form.
- If you owe taxes, staple your check or money order, on top of the W-2 form(s), to the original 1040EZ form.
- Send the original 1040EZ with Copy B of your W-2 form(s), plus any payment, to the Internal Revenue Service Center. Select the address from the list in your student activity text. Be sure to put enough postage on the envelope (you may need more than one stamp).

YOUR 1040EZ

Mention current forms

If you wish to complete a 1040EZ form for yourself, you should be aware that the forms and amounts in this book may not be accurate for the current year.

You may fill out the forms in this book for practice, but you should use a current form and use the amounts on that form when you prepare your taxes.

Refer to resources

Information on where to get help is in Chapter 8.

NOTE: You may wish to mention electronic filing (by computer). At this writing, some tax preparers now send the tax forms electronically, but a signature must still be sent through the mail. Plans are being made for complete electronic filing of tax returns in the near future.

IRS CENTERS

Alabama—Memphis, TN 37501

Alaska—Ogden, UT 84201

Arizona—Ogden, UT 84201

Arkansas—Memphis, TN 37501

California—*Counties of Alpine, Amador, Butts, Calaveras, Colusa, Contra Costa, Del Norte, El Dorado, Glenn, Humboldt, Lake, Lassen, Marin, Mendocino, Modoc, Napa, Nevada, Placer, Plumas, Sacramento, San Joaquin, Shasta, Sierra, Siskiyou, Solano, Sonoma, Sutter, Tehama, Trinity, Yolo, and Yuba*—Ogden, UT 84201

All other counties—Fresno, CA 93888

Colorado—Ogden, UT 84201

Connecticut—Andover, MA 05501

Delaware—Philadelphia, PA 19255

District of Columbia—Philadelphia, PA 19255

Florida—Atlanta, GA 39901

Georgia—Atlanta, GA 39901

Hawaii—Fresno, CA 93888

Idaho—Ogden, UT 84201

Illinois—Kansas City, MO 64999

Indiana—Cincinnati, OH 45999

Iowa—Kansas City, MO 64999

Kansas—Austin, TX 73301

Kentucky—Cincinnati, OH 45999

Louisiana—Memphis, TN 37501

Maine—Andover, MA 05501

Maryland—Philadelphia, PA 19255

Massachusetts—Andover, MA 05501

Michigan—Cincinnati, OH 45999

Minnesota—Kansas City, MO 64999

Mississippi—Memphis, TN 37501

Missouri—Kansas City, MO 64999

Montana—Ogden, UT 84201

Nebraska—Ogden, UT 84201

Nevada—Ogden, UT 84201

New Hampshire—Andover, MA 05501

New Jersey—Holtsville, NY 00501

New Mexico—Austin, TX 73301

New York—*New York City and counties of Nassau, Rockland, Suffolk, and Westchester*—Holtsville, NY 00501

All other counties—Andover, MA 05501

North Carolina—Memphis, TN 37501

North Dakota—Ogden, UT 84201

Ohio—Cincinnati, OH 45999

Oklahoma—Austin, TX 73301

Oregon—Ogden, UT 84201

Pennsylvania—Philadelphia, PA 19255

Rhode Island—Andover, MA 05501

South Carolina—Atlanta, GA 39901

South Dakota—Ogden, UT 84201

Tennessee—Memphis, TN 37501

Texas—Austin, TX 73301

Utah—Ogden, UT 84201

Vermont—Andover, MA 05501

Virginia—Philadelphia, PA 19255

Washington—Ogden, UT 84201

West Virginia—Cincinnati, OH 45999

Wisconsin—Kansas City, MO 64999

Wyoming—Ogden, UT 84201

American Samoa—Philadelphia, PA 19255

Guam—Commissioner of Revenue and Taxation
855 West Marine Dr.
Agana, GU 96910

Puerto Rico *(or if excluding income under section 933)*—Philadelphia, PA 19255

Virgin Islands: Nonpermanent residents—Philadelphia, PA 19255

Virgin Islands: Permanent residents—
V.I. Bureau of Internal Revenue
Lockharts Garden No. 1A
Charlotte Amalie
St. Thomas, VI 00802

Foreign country: *U.S. citizens and those filing Form 2555, Form 2555-EZ, or Form 4563*—Philadelphia, PA 19255

All A.P.O. and F.P.O. addresses—
Philadelphia, PA 19255

CHAPTER 7

Filling Out Forms—1040A

OVERVIEW

Topics

- Filling out the 1040A

Objectives

By the end of this chapter, the students will be able to:

- Fill out the 1040A tax return form.

Student activities

- Complete the 1040A.

Things you need

- You may wish to distribute copies of the 1040A form so that students can work with the form separately from the workbook. It will be easier to work with the form this way.

- If you will have students complete tax forms using their own information, they will need their tax information (see end of Chapter 5).

- Publication 17 will be useful for answering questions.

Important points

- The exercises in this chapter are based on 1998 information. This was the latest information available when the manuscript was completed. Be sure students understand this.

- Even if students will not use the 1040EZ, it is best to have them first complete the chapter on this form (Chapter 6), since it is simpler and allows them to build confi-

dence. However, if you do decide to omit Chapter 6, you should cover the vocabulary for that chapter.

- At the end of the exercise, you may wish to have participants repeat the exercises using tax forms for the current year. You will need to create you own answer keys.

- If you have participants complete the forms with their own tax information, you should use current forms, if available. Contact the IRS to inquire if a volunteer from VITA is available to assist you during this activity.

- Most people consider their financial situation highly personal. If students do not wish to reveal their own information, we recommend that you respect their wishes.

FILLING OUT FORMS— 1040A

Describe chapter

In this chapter, you will learn about:

- **Filling out the 1040A form.**

  We will go step by step through the form so that you understand each section.

  You will complete several practice exercises.

INSTRUCTIONS

Discuss instructions

- Read the information about the first sample taxpayer, Kim Tranh.

- Read the explanation of the 1040A form in this chapter.
- Complete the form for the first sample taxpayer using the information in the practice exercise.
- Complete the form for the other sample taxpayers using the information in the practice exercises at the end of this chapter.

NOTE: You can conduct this exercise in several ways.

For example, you can have students read the scenario about Kim Tranh and fill out the form as you review each section.

Alternatively, you can have students read the scenario, then review each section so that they understand it, and then complete the form at the end.

At the end of the chapter, additional scenarios address different situations.

COMPLETING THE 1040A—EXERCISE 1

ACTIVITY: Have students fill out the form for Kim Tranh's family. The next sections in this chapter have step-by-step instructions.

Describe taxpayers

Kim Tranh is a part-time waitress. Her husband, Viet, is a medical technician. Their daughter, Sun, is seven years old, and their son, Lee, is four.

Viet earned $24,800, and Kim earned $7,600, including tips.

They have no savings, and they have $2,500 in deductions.

Viet had $2,080 withheld from his pay, and Kim had $208 withheld from her pay.

They are not eligible to receive the earned income credit.

The Social Security numbers for the family are:

Kim:	987-65-4321
Viet:	001-34-3445
Sun:	002-22-9998
Lee:	002-45-9834

They live at 4300 Lakeview Avenue, Midville, TX 70000. They want to contribute to the Presidential Election Campaign fund.

Point out form

Your student activity text contains a blank copy of the 1040A form.

NOTE: The form is for the 1998 tax year.

1040A—PAGE 1

Form	Department of the Treasury–Internal Revenue Service		
1040A	**U.S. Individual Income Tax Return**	**1998**	IRS Use Only–Do not write or staple in this space.

OMB No. 1545-0085

Label
(See page 18.)

Use the IRS label.

Otherwise, please print or type.

L A B E L H E R E	Your first name and initial Viet	Last name Tranh	Your social security number 001 34 3445
	If a joint return, spouse's first name and initial Kim	Last name Tranh	Spouse's social security number 987 65 4321
	Home address (number and street). If you have a P.O. box, see page 19. 4300 Lakeview Avenue	Apt. no.	▲ IMPORTANT! ▲
	City, town or post office, state, and ZIP code. If you have a foreign address, see page 19. Midville, TX 70000		You **must** enter your SSN(s) above.

Presidential Election Campaign Fund (See page 19.)

		Yes	No
Do you want $3 to go to this fund?		☒	
If a joint return, does your spouse want $3 to go to this fund?		☒	

Note: *Checking "Yes" will not change your tax or reduce your refund.*

Filing status

Check only one box.

1 ☐ Single
2 ☒ Married filing joint return (even if only one had income)
3 ☐ Married filing separate return. Enter spouse's social security number above and full name here. ▶ _____
4 ☐ Head of household (with qualifying person). (See page 20.) If the qualifying person is a child but not your dependent, enter this child's name here. ▶ _____
5 ☐ Qualifying widow(er) with dependent child (year spouse died ▶ 19___). (See page 21.)

Exemptions

If more than seven dependents, see page 21.

6a ☒ **Yourself.** If your parent (or someone else) can claim you as a dependent on his or her tax return, **do not** check box 6a.

b ☒ **Spouse**

No. of boxes checked on 6a and 6b	2

c **Dependents:**

(1) First name Last name	(2) Dependent's social security number	(3) Dependent's relationship to you	(4) ✓ if qualified child for child tax credit (see page 22)
Sun Tranh	002 22 9998	daughter	☑
Lee Tranh	002 45 9834	son	☑
			☐
			☐
			☐
			☐
			☐

No. of your children on 6c who:	
• lived with you	2
• did not live with you due to divorce or separation (see page 23)	0
Dependents on 6c not entered above	0

d Total number of exemptions claimed.

Add numbers entered on lines above	4

Income

Attach Copy B of your Forms W-2 and 1099-R here.

If you did not get a W-2, see page 24.

Enclose, but do not staple, any payment.

7	Wages, salaries, tips, etc. Attach Form(s) W-2.	7	32,400	00
8a	**Taxable** interest. Attach Schedule 1 if required.	8a	0	00
b	**Tax-exempt** interest. DO NOT include on line 8a. 8b 0 00			
9	Ordinary dividends. Attach Schedule 1 if required.	9	0	00
10a	Total IRA distributions. 10a	10b Taxable amount (see page 24). 10b	0	00
11a	Total pensions and annuities. 11a	11b Taxable amount (see page 25). 11b	0	00
12	Unemployment compensation.	12	0	00
13a	Social security benefits. 13a	13b Taxable amount (see page 27). 13b	0	00
14	Add lines 7 through 13b (far right column). This is your **total income.** ▶	14	32,400	00

Adjusted gross income

15	IRA deduction (see page 28). 15 0 00			
16	Student loan interest deduction (see page 28). 16 0 00			
17	Add lines 15 and 16. These are your **total adjustments.**	17	0	00
18	Subtract line 17 from line 14. This is your **adjusted gross income.** If under $30,095 (under $10,030 if a child did not live with you), see the EIC instructions on page 36. ▶	18	32,400	00

For Disclosure, Privacy Act, and Paperwork Reduction Act Notice, see page 49.   Cat. No. 11327A   **1998 Form 1040A**

1040A—PAGE 2

1998 Form 1040A page 2

Taxable income	**19**	Enter the amount from line 18.	**19**	32,400 00

20a Check if: □ **You** were 65 or older □ Blind } □ **Spouse** was 65 or older □ Blind } Enter number of boxes checked ▶ **20a** | 0 |

b If you are married filing separately and your spouse itemizes deductions, see page 30 and check here . . . . . . ▶ **20b** □

21 Enter the **standard deduction** for your filing status. **But** see page 31 if you checked any box on line 20a or 20b **OR** if someone can claim you as a dependent.
- Single—$4,250 • Married filing jointly or Qualifying widow(er)—$7,100
- Head of household—$6,250 • Married filing separately—$3,550 | **21** | 7,100 00 |

22	Subtract line 21 from line 19. If line 21 is more than line 19, enter -0-.	**22**	25,300 00
23	Multiply $2,700 by the total number of exemptions claimed on line 6d.	**23**	10,800 00
24	Subtract line 23 from line 22. If line 23 is more than line 22, enter -0-. This is your **taxable income.** ▶	**24**	14,500 00

Tax, credits, and payments	**25**	Find the tax on the amount on line 24 (see page 31).			**25**	2,179 00
	26	Credit for child and dependent care expenses. Attach Schedule 2.	**26**	0 00		
	27	Credit for the elderly or the disabled. Attach Schedule 3.	**27**	0 00		
	28	Child tax credit (see page 32).	**28**	800 00		
	29	Education credits. Attach Form 8863.	**29**	0 00		
	30	Adoption credit. Attach Form 8839.	**30**	0 00		
	31	Add lines 26 through 30. These are your **total credits.**			**31**	800 00
	32	Subtract line 31 from line 25. If line 31 is more than line 25, enter -0-.			**32**	1,379 00
	33	Advance earned income credit payments from Form(s) W-2.			**33**	0 00
	34	Add lines 32 and 33. This is your **total tax.** ▶			**34**	1,379 00
	35	Total Federal income tax withheld from Forms W-2 and 1099.	**35**	2,288 00		
	36	1998 estimated tax payments and amount applied from 1997 return.	**36**	0 00		
	37a	**Earned income credit.** Attach Schedule EIC if you have a qualifying child.	**37a**	0 00		
	b	Nontaxable earned income: amount ▶ and type ▶				
	38	Additional child tax credit. Attach Form 8812.	**38**	0 00		
	39	Add lines 35, 36, 37a, and 38. These are your **total payments.** ▶			**39**	2,288 00

Refund Have it directly deposited! See page 43 and fill in 41b, 41c, and 41d.	**40**	If line 39 is more than line 34, subtract line 34 from line 39. This is the amount you **overpaid.**		**40**	909 00
	41a	Amount of line 40 you want **refunded to you.**		**41a**	
	b	Routing number ☐☐☐☐☐☐☐☐☐ **c** Type: □ Checking □ Savings			
	d	Account number ☐☐☐☐☐☐☐☐☐☐☐☐☐☐☐☐☐			
	42	Amount of line 40 you want **applied to your 1999 estimated tax.**	**42**		

Amount you owe	**43**	If line 34 is more than line 39, subtract line 39 from line 34. This is the **amount you owe.** For details on how to pay, see page 44.	**43**	
	44	Estimated tax penalty (see page 44).	**44**	

Sign here

Joint return? See page 19.
Keep a copy for your records.

Under penalties of perjury, I declare that I have examined this return and accompanying schedules and statements, and to the best of my knowledge and belief, they are true, correct, and accurately list all amounts and sources of income I received during the tax year. Declaration of preparer (other than the taxpayer) is based on all information of which the preparer has any knowledge.

Your signature	Date	Your occupation Medical technician	Daytime telephone number (optional)
Spouse's signature. If joint return, BOTH must sign.	Date	Spouse's occupation waitress	( )

Paid preparer's use only

Preparer's signature ▶	Date	Check if self-employed □	Preparer's social security no.
Firm's name (or yours if self-employed) and address ▶			EIN :
			ZIP code

✸

1040A—CHILD TAX CREDIT WORKSHEET

Child Tax Credit Worksheet–Line 28

▶ Keep for your records.

Do Not File

1. $400.00 ___**2**___ . Multiply and enter the result . . . . . . 1. **800|00**

   Enter number of qualifying children (see page 32)

2. Enter the amount from Form 1040A, line 19 . . . . . 2. **32,400|00**

3. Is line 2 above more than $55,000?

   ☒ **No.** Skip lines 3 through 5, enter -0- on line 6, and go to line 7.

   ☐ **Yes.** Enter: $75,000 if single, head of household, or qualifying widow(er); $110,000 if married filing jointly; $55,000 if married filing separately . . . . . 3. _____

4. Subtract line 3 from line 2. If zero or less, enter -0- here and on line 6, and go to line 7 . . . . 4. _____

5. Divide line 4 by $1,000. If the result is not a whole number, round it up to the next higher whole number (for example, round 0.01 to 1) . . . . 5. _____

6. Multiply $50 by the number on line 5 . . . . 6. **0|00**

7. Subtract line 6 from line 1. If zero or less, **stop here; you cannot** take this credit . 7. **800|00**

8. Enter the amount from Form 1040A, line 25 . . . . . 8. **2,179|00**

9. Is line 1 above more than $800?

   ☒ **No.** Add the amounts from Form 1040A, lines 26, 27, and 29. Enter the total.

   ☐ **Yes.** Enter the amount from the worksheet on page 34. ⎬ 9. **0|00**

10. Subtract line 9 above from line 8 . . . . 10. **2,179|00**

11. **Child tax credit.** Enter the **smaller** of line 7 or line 10 here and on Form 1040A, line 28 ▶ 11. **800|00**

TIP *If line 1 above is more than $800, you may be able to take the **Additional Child Tax Credit**. See page 32.*

WHO CAN USE THE 1040A?

Identify requirements

The 1040A is for taxpayers of any age with:

☐ A total taxable income of $50,000 or less.

☐ Any amount of taxable interest or dividend income.

☐ Any filing status.

☐ Any number of dependents.

Unacceptable income sources:

☐ Rental income.

☐ Income from own business or contract work.

ACTIVITY: If you want to determine if you can use the 1040A, place a check in each box that applies to your situation. If you check *all* the boxes, you can use the 1040A.

Ask questions

1. What are the differences between requirements for the 1040EZ and the 1040A?

<u>On the 1040EZ:</u>

- The maximum taxable interest income allowed is $400.

- Only the single and married filing jointly filing statuses are permitted (for sighted people under 65).

- Dependents cannot be claimed.

<u>On the 1040A:</u>

- Any amount of interest income is allowed.

- Any filing status is permitted.

- Dependents can be claimed.

The maximum taxable income limit is the same ($50,000) for both forms.

2. Can Kim Tranh's family use the 1040A?

Yes.

- Their income is less than $50,000.

SECTION 1: NAME AND ADDRESS

Introduce Section 1

In this initial section of the 1040A form, you print personal information.

Form **1040A**	Department of the Treasury–Internal Revenue Service **U.S. Individual Income Tax Return**	**1998**	IRS Use Only–Do not write or staple in this space.

Label

(See page 18.)

Use the IRS label.

Otherwise, please print or type.

L A B E L H E R E

Your first name and initial	Last name	Your social security number
If a joint return, spouse's first name and initial	Last name	Spouse's social security number

OMB No. 1545-0085

Home address (number and street). If you have a P.O. box, see page 19.	Apt. no.

▲ **IMPORTANT!** ▲

You **must** enter your SSN(s) above.

City, town or post office, state, and ZIP code. If you have a foreign address, see page 19.

Presidential Election Campaign Fund (See page 19.)
Do you want $3 to go to this fund? . . . .
If a joint return, does your spouse want $3 to go to this fund?

Yes	No

Note: *Checking "Yes" will not change your tax or reduce your refund.*

Mention label

If you received your form in the mail, it may have a label attached; place the label on this section. Otherwise, print the information.

- **In the large rectangle, print:**

  Your first name, initial, and last (family) name.

  Your spouse's first name, initial, and last (family) name, if applicable.

  Home address: number, street, and apartment number.

  City, state, and ZIP code.

- **At the right of the large rectangle, print your Social Security number. Also print your spouse's Social Security number if you are married.**

NOTE: If students are originally from other countries, it is important that they understand the appropriate way to complete the form. Names and addresses are written differently in other countries.

Presidential Election Campaign contribution

In this section, you and your spouse must decide whether you want the IRS to contribute $3.00 of your tax money to a special fund to help pay for presidential election costs.

This will not increase your tax owed or decrease the amount of your refund. The money the IRS contributes to this fund is money that you have already paid.

- Mark an X in the first Yes box if you do want the IRS to contribute $3.00 to the special fund. Or mark an X in the first No box if you do *not* want the IRS to contribute $3.00 to the special fund.

- Mark an X in the second Yes box if your spouse does want the IRS to contribute $3.00 to the special fund. Or mark an X in the second No box if your spouse does *not* want the IRS to contribute $3.00 to the special fund.

SECTION 2: FILING STATUS

Introduce Section 2

In this section of the 1040A, you must indicate your filing status. As discussed in Chapter 4, there are five types of filing status:

1. Single.

2. Married filing joint return.

3. Married filing separate return.

4. Head of household.

5. Qualifying widow(er) with dependent child.

Filing status		
	1 ☐	Single
	2 ☐	Married filing joint return (even if only one had income)
	3 ☐	Married filing separate return. Enter spouse's social security number above and full name here. ▶ _____
Check only one box.	**4** ☐	Head of household (with qualifying person). (See page 20.) If the qualifying person is a child but not your dependent, enter this child's name here. ▶ _____
	5 ☐	Qualifying widow(er) with dependent child (year spouse died ▶ 19____). (See page 21.)

Mark the correct box

Mark an X in the appropriate box.

- If you marked an X in box 3, print your spouse's full name in the space provided. Enter your spouse's Social Security number in the space provided at the top of the form.

- If you marked an X in box 4 and the qualifying person is a child who is not your dependent, print the child's name in the space provided.

NOTE: The preceding is a very unusual situation.

- If you marked an X in box 5, print the year your spouse died in the space provided.

  The spouse must have died within the previous two tax years for the taxpayer to be considered a qualifying widow(er).

SECTION 3: YOUR EXEMPTIONS

Introduce Section 3

In this section of the 1040A, where you figure your exemptions, you must print personal information about yourself and your dependents.

Exemptions					
	6a ☐ **Yourself.** If your parent (or someone else) can claim you as a dependent on his or her tax return, **do not** check box 6a.				**No. of boxes checked on 6a and 6b** ____
	b ☐ **Spouse**				
	c Dependents:	**(2)** Dependent's social security number	**(3)** Dependent's relationship to you	**(4)** ✔ if qualified child for child tax credit (see page 22)	**No. of your children on 6c who:**
	(1) First name Last name				• **lived with you** ____
If more than seven dependents, see page 21.	_____	____:____	_____	☐	• **did not live with you due to divorce or separation (see page 23)** ____
	_____	____:____	_____	☐	
	_____	____:____	_____	☐	
	_____	____:____	_____	☐	**Dependents on 6c not entered above** ____
	_____	____:____	_____	☐	
	_____	____:____	_____	☐	
	_____	____:____	_____	☐	**Add numbers entered on lines above** ☐
	d Total number of exemptions claimed.				

6a. If you were not claimed as a dependent on someone else's income tax return, mark an X in box 6a.

6b. If you were married and are filing jointly, mark an X in box 6b.

6c. On the lines under box 6c, print:

- First and last (family) names of all your dependents (column 1).

- Social Security number of each dependent (column 2).

- The dependent's relationship to you (column 3).

- An X in the box, if the dependent is under age 17 AND is your son, daughter, adopted child, grandchild, stepchild, or foster child AND is a U.S. citizen (column 4).

- Look at the lines on the right side of the form in this section.

  On the top line, print the total number of boxes marked in 6a and 6b (0, 1, or 2).

  On the next line, to the right of 6c, print the number of your children who lived with you.

- On the next line, print the number of your children who did not live with you because of divorce or separation.

- On the next line, print the number of other dependents listed in 6c.

- Add the number of exemptions claimed in 6a, 6b, and 6c.

6d. Print the total in the box to the right of 6d. This is the number of exemptions you can claim.

SECTION 4: FIGURING TOTAL INCOME

Introduce Section 4

In this section of the 1040A, you must print financial information about your income. This information includes:

- Total wages, salaries, and tips.
- Total taxable interest income.
- Total IRA and pension income.
- Unemployment compensation income.
- Social Security income.

Point out usual situation

Most people have only a few types of income.

Mention writing 0

If you do not have the types of income that must be recorded, simply write a 0 (zero).

Provide example

If you are a young working person, you probably do not receive Social Security income. When the form asks how much you receive in Social Security benefits, you would simply write a zero.

Income			
	7 Wages, salaries, tips, etc. Attach Form(s) W-2.	**7**	
Attach Copy B of your Forms W-2 and 1099-R here.	**8a Taxable** interest. Attach Schedule 1 if required.	**8a**	
	b Tax-exempt interest. DO NOT include on line 8a. **8b**		
	9 Ordinary dividends. Attach Schedule 1 if required.	**9**	
	10a Total IRA distributions. **10a**	**10b** Taxable amount (see page 24). **10b**	
If you did not get a W-2, see page 24.	**11a** Total pensions and annuities. **11a**	**11b** Taxable amount (see page 25). **11b**	
Enclose, but do not staple, any payment.	**12** Unemployment compensation.	**12**	
	13a Social security benefits. **13a**	**13b** Taxable amount (see page 27). **13b**	
	14 Add lines 7 through 13b (far right column). This is your **total income**. ▶ **14**		

7. Add up total wages, salaries, and tips. Print the total on line 7.

   • Refer to W-2 form(s) for the totals.

   • You will have to attach the W-2 form(s) to the 1040A.

8. Add up total taxable interest. Refer to 1099-INT form(s).

   • In 8a, print the total. (If the total exceeds $400, you must also complete Schedule 1. See the Appendix.)

   • Add up total tax-exempt interest. In 8b, print the total.

9. Add up dividends. Print the total in the space on line 9. (If the total exceeds $400, you must also complete Schedule 1. See the Appendix.)

10a. Add up total IRA income. In 10a, print the total.

10b. Add up total taxable IRA income. In 10b, print the total.

11a. Add up the total pension income. In 11a, print the total.

11b. Add up the total taxable pension income. In 11b, print the total.

12. Add up the total unemployment compensation income. On line 12, print the total.

13a. Add up the total Social Security income. In 13a, print the total.

13b. Add up the total taxable Social Security income. In 13b, print the total.

Figure total income

On line 14, add up all the types of income you have and record the total.

14.   Add the amounts on lines 7, 8a, 9, 10b, 11b, 12, and 13b. Print the total on line 14.

  •   This amount is your total income.

SECTION 5: ADJUSTED GROSS INCOME

Introduce Section 5

In this section, you calculate your adjusted gross income. If you have an IRA, you must first total the amount of IRA deduction that will reduce your taxable income.

Adjusted gross income	15	IRA deduction (see page 28).	15	
	16	Student loan interest deduction (see page 28).	16	
	17	Add lines 15 and 16. These are your **total adjustments.**	17	
	18	Subtract line 17 from line 14. This is your **adjusted gross income.** If under $30,095 (under $10,030 if a child did not live with you), see the EIC instructions on page 36.	▶ 18	

For Disclosure, Privacy Act, and Paperwork Reduction Act Notice, see page 49.   Cat. No. 11327A   **1998 Form 1040A**

NOTE: The adjusted gross income is the total gross income less certain excludable (tax-exempt) items allowed and defined by the federal government.

Mention skipping to 16

If you do not have an IRA, skip to line 16.

NOTE: There is a separate worksheet taxpayers can use to calculate their IRA deductions. This is because there are rules about how much you can deduct for IRAs. This worksheet is used to calculate the correct amount.

---

15.   Add up your total IRA deduction. Print the total in space 15.

16.   You may be eligible for a student loan interest deduction. If you paid interest on a student loan during the past year, refer to the instructions provided with the 1040A to see if you qualified and to fill out the student loan interest deduction worksheet.

   If you qualified, print the amount from the worksheet on line 16.

   If you did not qualify, print 0 on line 16.

NOTE: Instructions for the student loan interest deduction worksheet are not provided with these materials.

17. Add the amounts on lines 15 and 16 (line 15 + line 16). Print the result on line 17. These are **total adjustments.**

18. Subtract the amount on line 17 from line 14 (line 14 – line 17). Print the result on line 18.

    • This is your **adjusted gross income.**

    • If this amount is less than $30,095, you should see the information on earned income credit (EIC) in the Appendix of this book. You may be able to pay less tax.

NOTE: For now, continue reviewing the steps as if the EIC did not apply. You may address this topic in the Appendix.

SECTION 6: FIGURING DEDUCTIONS

Introduce Section 6

In this section of the 1040A, you must total the amount of deductions and subtract that amount from your total income.

1998 Form 1040A page 2

Taxable income		
19	Enter the amount from line 18.	19
20a	Check if: ☐ **You** were 65 or older ☐ Blind ☐ **Spouse** was 65 or older ☐ Blind **Enter number of boxes checked ▶** 20a ☐	
b	If you are married filing separately and your spouse itemizes deductions, see page 30 and check here . . . . . ▶ 20b ☐	
21	Enter the **standard deduction** for your filing status. **But** see page 31 if you checked any box on line 20a or 20b **OR** if someone can claim you as a dependent. • Single—$4,250 • Married filing jointly or Qualifying widow(er)—$7,100 • Head of household—$6,250 • Married filing separately—$3,550 21	
22	Subtract line 21 from line 19. If line 21 is more than line 19, enter -0-. 22	
23	Multiply $2,700 by the total number of exemptions claimed on line 6d. 23	
24	Subtract line 23 from line 22. If line 23 is more than line 22, enter -0-. This is your **taxable income.** ▶ 24	

19. Print the amount from line 18 on line 19.

20a. Mark an X in the small boxes if:

    • You are 65 or older.

    • Your spouse is 65 or older.

- You are blind.

- Your spouse is blind.

Count the number of boxes marked with an X. Print the total in the big box to the right of 20a.

20b. If you are married filing separately AND your spouse files Form 1040 AND your spouse itemizes his or her deductions, mark an X in box 20b.

21. Enter the correct amount of the standard deduction for your filing status. The amounts are shown on the form.

- If you check any boxes in 20, or if someone can claim you as a dependent on his or her income tax, be sure to follow the special instructions.

22. Subtract the amount in 21 from the amount in 19 (line 19 – line 21) and print the result on line 22.

- If the amount on line 21 is more than the amount on line 19, print 0 on line 22.

23. Multiply $2,700 times the amount on line 6d ($2,700 × line 6d) and print the result on line 23.

NOTE: This amount is likely to change from year to year.

---

24. Subtract the amount on line 23 from the amount on line 22 (line 22 – line 23) and print the result on line 24.

- If the amount on line 23 is more than the amount on line 22, print 0 on line 24.

- The amount on line 24 is your taxable income.

SECTION 7: TAX, CREDITS, PAYMENTS

Introduce Section 7

In this section, you must look up your tax in the tax tables and total the amount of your credits. These credits include:

- Credits for child-care expenses.
- Federal income tax withheld from your paychecks.
- Earned income credit for low-income taxpayers.

Tax, credits, and payments	**25**	Find the tax on the amount on line 24 (see page 31).		25
	26	Credit for child and dependent care expenses. Attach Schedule 2.	26	
	27	Credit for the elderly or the disabled. Attach Schedule 3.	27	
	28	Child tax credit (see page 32).	28	
	29	Education credits. Attach Form 8863.	29	
	30	Adoption credit. Attach Form 8839.	30	
	31	Add lines 26 through 30. These are your **total credits.**		31
	32	Subtract line 31 from line 25. If line 31 is more than line 25, enter -0-.		32
	33	Advance earned income credit payments from Form(s) W-2.		33
	34	Add lines 32 and 33. This is your **total tax.**	▶	34
	35	Total Federal income tax withheld from Forms W-2 and 1099.	35	
	36	1998 estimated tax payments and amount applied from 1997 return.	36	
	37a	**Earned income credit.** Attach Schedule EIC if you have a qualifying child.	37a	
	b	Nontaxable earned income: amount ▶ and type ▶		
	38	Additional child tax credit. Attach Form 8812.	38	
	39	Add lines 35, 36, 37a, and 38. These are your **total payments.**	▶	39

Select tax tables

25. Look in the tax tables. Find your taxable income (line 24). Print the amount of tax on line 25.

NOTE: Tax tables are included at the back of the student activity text and this teacher guide. Each year, the tables are updated and provided with the annually revised tax forms.

Describe lines 26–31

Items 26–31 are used to calculate your total credits. You can get credits for child care expenses, for adoption expenses, for education expenses, or for being an elderly or disabled person.

26. If you had child-care expenses, you must include the form Schedule 2 with your 1040A. (See the Appendix for instructions.)

   • On line 26, write the amount of credit for child-care expenses from Schedule 2, line 9. If you had no child-care expenses, print 0 (zero) on line 26.

NOTE: We recommend that you continue with the discussion of this form and cover Schedule 2 in the Appendix during a separate session.

---

27. If you were an elderly or disabled person, you must include the form Schedule 3 with your 1040A.

   • On line 27, write the amount of this credit from Schedule 3. If you had no elderly or disabled person care credits, print 0 on line 27.

NOTE: Instructions for this schedule are not included in these materials.

---

28. If you did not have a qualifying child, print 0 on line 28 and continue to line 29.

   If you had a child who qualified for a tax credit, you will need to fill out the Child Tax Credit Worksheet. This worksheet should not be submitted with the 1040A, but it should be kept for your own records.

   On line 28, write the child tax credit from line 11 of the Child Tax Credit Worksheet.

Child Tax Credit Worksheet–Line 28

Do Not File

► Keep for your records.

1. $400.00 _____ . Multiply and enter the result . . . . . . 1. _____

   ▲ Enter number of qualifying children (see page 32)

2. Enter the amount from Form 1040A, line 19 . . . . . 2. _____

3. Is line 2 above more than $55,000?

   ☐ **No.** Skip lines 3 through 5, enter -0- on line 6, and go to line 7.

   ☐ **Yes.** Enter: $75,000 if single, head of household, or qualifying widow(er); $110,000 if married filing jointly; $55,000 if married filing separately . . . . . 3. _____

4. Subtract line 3 from line 2. If zero or less, enter -0- here and on line 6, and go to line 7 . . . . 4. _____

5. Divide line 4 by $1,000. If the result is not a whole number, round it up to the next higher whole number (for example, round 0.01 to 1) . . . . 5. _____

6. Multiply $50 by the number on line 5 . . . . 6. _____

7. Subtract line 6 from line 1. If zero or less, **stop here; you cannot** take this credit . 7. _____

8. Enter the amount from Form 1040A, line 25 . . . . . 8. _____

9. Is line 1 above more than $800?

   ☐ **No.** Add the amounts from Form 1040A, lines 26, 27, and 29. Enter the total.

   ☐ **Yes.** Enter the amount from the worksheet on page 34. ⎬ 9. _____

10. Subtract line 9 above from line 8 . . . . 10. _____

11. **Child tax credit.** Enter the **smaller** of line 7 or line 10 here and on Form 1040A, line 28 ► 11. _____

TIP *If line 1 above is more than $800, you may be able to take the **Additional Child Tax Credit**. See page 32.*

----

1. In part 1, write the number of qualifying children you have. Multiply this number by 400 and write the answer on line 1.

2. On line 2, enter the amount from line 19 of Form 1040A.

3. If line 2 if less than $55,000 check No and skip lines 3 through 5. Write 0 on line 6 and continue on to line 7.

    If line 2 is greater than $55,000 check Yes and enter the appropriate amount on line 3.

4. Subtract line 3 from line 2 (line 3 – line 2). If line 2 is larger than line 3, write 0 on lines 4 and 5 and go to line 7.

5. Divide line 4 by $1,000. If the result is not a whole number, round it up to the next whole number. Write the answer on line 5.

6. Multiply line 5 by $50 and write the result on line 6.

7. Subtract line 6 from line 1 (line 1 – line 6). If line 6 is greater than line 1, STOP—you cannot take this credit. If line 1 is greater than line 6, write the remainder on line 7.

8. Write the amount from line 25 of Form 1040A.

9. If line 1 is greater than $800, check Yes. You will need to fill out another worksheet, which can be found in the instructions for the 1040A. If line 1 is $800 or less, check No. Add the amounts from lines 26, 27, and 29 on Form 1040A. Write the sum on line 9.

10. Subtract line 9 from line 8 (line 9 – line 8). Write the result on line 10.

11. Look at line 7 and line 10. Write the smaller number on line 11 and on Form 1040A, line 28.

----

29. If you had post-secondary education expenses, you may qualify for education credits. Include Form 8863 with your return.

    - On line 29, write the amount of this credit from Form 8863. If you were not eligible for education credits, print 0 on line 29.

30. If you had adoption expenses, you must include Form 8839 with your 1040A.

    - On line 30, write the amount of this credit from Form 8839. If you had no adoption expenses, print 0 on line 30.

NOTE: Instructions for these forms are not included in these materials.

---

31. Add the figures from lines 26 through 30. Print the total on line 31.

    - These are your **total credits.**

Go over lines 32 and 33

32. Subtract the amount on line 31 from the amount on line 25 (25 – 31) and print the result on line 32.

   • If line 31 is more than line 25, print 0 (zero).

33. Add the amounts from box 9 on each of your W-2 forms. Print the total on line 33.

NOTE: Advance earned income credit payments can be received by people who know they will be eligible for the earned income credit (EIC). If students want to know more about this, they should ask their employers.

Describe line 34

On line 34, you will calculate your total tax.

34. Add the amounts on lines 32 and 33. Print the total on line 34.

   • This amount is your **total tax.**

Describe lines 34–39

In lines 34 to 39, you will determine your total payments—that is, the amount of taxes you have already paid by withholding. If you are entitled to earned income credit (EIC), this amount is included as part of the total tax payment.

35. Add the amounts from box 2 on each of your W-2 forms and print the total on line 35.

36. If you sent estimated tax payments (for example, if you had a large interest income), add the total of these payments and print the amount on line 36. If you had no estimated tax payments, print 0 on line 36.

37a. If you earned less than $30,095 AND line 18 on the 1040A form is less than $30,095, you may be eligible to receive an earned income credit. If you have at least one **dependent child,** you must complete the Schedule EIC form (see the Appendix) and print the amount from the earned income credit worksheet on line 37a. Otherwise, print 0 (zero) on line 37a.

37b. Certain types of income are not taxable, but you must include them on your tax return to see if you can receive the earned income credit. Examples of nontaxable earned income are housing allowances or meals and lodging provided by your employer or the military.

   If you received nontaxable earned income from your employer, write the amount and type on line 37b.

NOTE: Welfare, SSI, and Food Stamps are not earned income. Do not include them in 37b.

---

38. If you qualified for a Child Tax Credit, you may be eligible for an additional child tax credit. It is necessary to fill out Form 8812 to calculate the credit. Write this amount on line 38. If you do not qualify write 0 on line 38.

NOTE: Instructions for Form 8812 are not included in these materials.

---

39. Add the amounts on lines 35, 36, 37a, and 38. Print the total on line 39.

   • This is your **total tax payment.**

SECTION 8: REFUND OR TAXES OWED

Introduce Section 8

In this section of the 1040A, you must compare the amount of tax credits and payments with the amount of taxes owed. This will determine whether you receive a refund or if you must pay more taxes.

Refund	40	If line 39 is more than line 34, subtract line 34 from line 39. This is the amount you **overpaid.**	40	
Have it directly deposited! See page 43 and fill in 41b, 41c, and 41d.	41a	Amount of line 40 you want **refunded to you.**	41a	
	b	Routing number ⬚⬚⬚⬚⬚⬚⬚⬚⬚ **c** Type: ☐ Checking ☐ Savings		
	d	Account number ⬚⬚⬚⬚⬚⬚⬚⬚⬚⬚⬚⬚⬚⬚⬚⬚⬚		
	42	Amount of line 40 you want **applied to your 1999 estimated tax.** 42		
Amount you owe	43	If line 34 is more than line 39, subtract line 39 from line 34. This is the **amount you owe.** For details on how to pay, see page 44.	43	
	44	Estimated tax penalty (see page 44). 44		

40. Look to see if the amount on line 39 is larger than the amount on line 34. If it is smaller, go to line 43. If it is larger, then subtract the amount on line 34 from the amount on line 39 (line 34 – line 39). Print the result on line 40.

   • You have paid too much in taxes and can receive a refund for this amount.

Introduce lines 41, 42, and 43

If you have paid too much in taxes, you have a choice of either receiving the refund (line 41a) or applying all or part of the refund to the next year's taxes (line 42).

41a. Print the number from line 40 on line 41a if you want the money refunded to you. (Most people prefer this.)

   The IRS will now directly deposit your refund in the bank if you have a checking or savings account. This is a good idea because it prevents lost or stolen income tax refund checks. If you prefer to receive a refund check, leave 41b, 41c, and 41d blank.

41b. Print the routing number of your bank. (Ask the bank for this nine-digit number.)

41c. Put an X in the correct box to indicate whether your income tax refund is to be deposited into your checking or savings account.

41d. Write your account number in the boxes.

42. You can have all or part of your refund applied to the next year's taxes. If you prefer to receive the refund, print 0 (zero) on line 42.

43. If the amount on line 39 is smaller than the amount on line 34, then subtract the amount on line 39 from the amount on line 34 (line 34 – line 39). Print the result on line 43.

   • You owe this amount of taxes to the IRS.

   • Prepare a check or money order, payable to the IRS, for this amount.

   • Print your name, address, Social Security number, daytime telephone number, and "199_ Form 1040A" on the check or money order.

44. Write a 0 (zero) on line 44 unless you owe a penalty. Refer to the instructions on the form regarding penalties.

NOTE: 199_ is used to indicate that the students should write the current tax year on their check or money orders. For example, if they are filing on April 15, 1999, they would write "1998 Form 1040A" on their check or money order.

SECTION 9: SIGNING YOUR RETURN

Introduce Section 9

In this final section of the 1040A, you (and your spouse) must sign and date your income tax report. You must also indicate your occupation(s).

Sign here	Under penalties of perjury, I declare that I have examined this return and accompanying schedules and statements, and to the best of my knowledge and belief, they are true, correct, and accurately list all amounts and sources of income I received during the tax year. Declaration of preparer (other than the taxpayer) is based on all information of which the preparer has any knowledge.			
Joint return? See page 19. Keep a copy for your records.	Your signature	Date	Your occupation	Daytime telephone number (optional)
	Spouse's signature. If joint return, BOTH must sign.	Date	Spouse's occupation	( )
Paid preparer's use only	Preparer's signature	Date	Check if self-employed ☐	Preparer's social security no.
	Firm's name (or yours if self-employed) and address			EIN ⋮
				ZIP code

- In the area that says "Your signature," sign your name.
- In the area that says "Spouse's signature" (if a joint return, both must sign), have your spouse sign, if applicable.
- Print the date beside each signature.
- Print the occupation beside each date.

Paid preparer

- If you paid a person to prepare your taxes, that person must fill in this section. Otherwise, leave it blank.

1040A FINAL PROCEDURES

Identify final steps

The final things to do once you have completed the form are:
- Make a copy of this form for your records.
- Staple Copy B of your W-2 form(s) to the original 1040A form.
- If you owe taxes, staple your check or money order, on top of the W-2 form(s), to the original 1040A form.
- Send Copy B of the W-2 form(s) and the original 1040A, plus any payment, to your Internal Revenue Service Center. Select the address from the list in your student activity text.

NOTE: You may wish to mention electronic filing (by computer). At this writing, some tax preparers now send the tax forms electronically, but a signature must still be sent through the mail. Plans are being made for complete electronic filing of tax returns in the near future.

YOUR 1040A

Mention current forms

If you wish to complete a 1040A form for yourself, you should be aware that the forms and amounts in this book may not be accurate for the current year.

You can fill out the forms in this book for practice, but you should use a current form and use the amounts on that form when you prepare your taxes.

Refer to resources

- Information on where to get help is in Chapter 8.

COMPLETING THE 1040A—EXERCISE 2

ACTIVITY: Have students fill out the form for Mary Wong's family.

Describe taxpayer

Mary Wong is a bookkeeper. Her husband died four years ago, and she has not remarried. Her son, Daniel, is six years old.

She earned $27,692 in 1998. Her savings account at the bank earned $100 in interest.

Her deductions total $3,000. She had $3,094 withheld from her year's earnings.

Their Social Security numbers are:

Mary: 987-33-1234

Daniel: 777-32-4503

They live at 12 Mountain Drive, Apt. 7D, Stoneplain, NY 10000. She wants to contribute to the Presidential Election Campaign fund.

1040A FOR MARY WONG—PAGE 1

Form **1040A**	Department of the Treasury–Internal Revenue Service **U.S. Individual Income Tax Return**	**1998**	IRS Use Only–Do not write or staple in this space.

Label
(See page 18.)

Use the IRS label.
Otherwise, please print or type.

OMB No. 1545-0085

L A B E L   H E R E

Your first name and initial **Mary**   Last name **Wong**

Your social security number **987 33 1234**

If a joint return, spouse's first name and initial   Last name

Spouse's social security number

Home address (number and street). If you have a P.O. box, see page 19. **12 Mountain Drive**   Apt. no. **7D**

City, town or post office, state, and ZIP code. If you have a foreign address, see page 19. **Stoneplain, NY 10000**

▲ **IMPORTANT!** ▲
You **must** enter your SSN(s) above.

Presidential Election Campaign Fund (See page 19.)
Do you want $3 to go to this fund? . . . .
If a joint return, does your spouse want $3 to go to this fund?

	Yes	No
	✗	

Note: Checking "Yes" will not change your tax or reduce your refund.

Filing status

Check only one box.

1. ☐ Single
2. ☐ Married filing joint return (even if only one had income)
3. ☐ Married filing separate return. Enter spouse's social security number above and full name here. ▶ _____
4. ☒ Head of household (with qualifying person). (See page 20.) If the qualifying person is a child but not your dependent, enter this child's name here. ▶ _____
5. ☐ Qualifying widow(er) with dependent child (year spouse died ▶ 19___). (See page 21.)

Exemptions

If more than seven dependents, see page 21.

6a ☒ **Yourself.** If your parent (or someone else) can claim you as a dependent on his or her tax return, **do not** check box 6a.

b ☐ **Spouse**

c **Dependents:**

(1) First name Last name	(2) Dependent's social security number	(3) Dependent's relationship to you	(4) ✔ if qualified child for child tax credit (see page 22)
Daniel Wong	777 32 4503	son	✔
			☐
			☐
			☐
			☐
			☐
			☐

No. of boxes checked on 6a and 6b **1**

No. of your children on 6c who:
• lived with you **1**
• did not live with you due to divorce or separation (see page 23) **0**

Dependents on 6c not entered above **0**

Add numbers entered on lines above **2**

d Total number of exemptions claimed.

Income

Attach Copy B of your Forms W-2 and 1099-R here.

If you did not get a W-2, see page 24.

Enclose, but do not staple, any payment.

7	Wages, salaries, tips, etc. Attach Form(s) W-2.	7	27,692 00
8a	**Taxable** interest. Attach Schedule 1 if required.	8a	100 00
b	**Tax-exempt** interest. DO NOT include on line 8a. 8b 0 00		
9	Ordinary dividends. Attach Schedule 1 if required.	9	0 00
10a	Total IRA distributions. 10a	10b Taxable amount (see page 24). 10b	0 00
11a	Total pensions and annuities. 11a	11b Taxable amount (see page 25). 11b	0 00
12	Unemployment compensation.	12	0 00
13a	Social security benefits. 13a	13b Taxable amount (see page 27). 13b	0 00
14	Add lines 7 through 13b (far right column). This is your **total income.** ▶	14	27,792 00

Adjusted gross income

15	IRA deduction (see page 28). 15 0 00		
16	Student loan interest deduction (see page 28). 16 0 00		
17	Add lines 15 and 16. These are your **total adjustments.**	17	0 00
18	Subtract line 17 from line 14. This is your **adjusted gross income.** If under $30,095 (under $10,030 if a child did not live with you), see the EIC instructions on page 36. ▶	18	27,792 00

For Disclosure, Privacy Act, and Paperwork Reduction Act Notice, see page 49.   Cat. No. 11327A   **1998 Form 1040A**

1040A FOR MARY WONG—PAGE 2

1998 Form 1040A page 2

Taxable income	**19**	Enter the amount from line 18.	19	27,792 00

20a Check if: ☐ **You** were 65 or older ☐ Blind ☐ **Spouse** was 65 or older ☐ Blind } **Enter number of boxes checked ▶** 20a ☐

b If you are married filing separately and your spouse itemizes deductions, see page 30 and check here . . . . . . ▶ 20b ☐

21 Enter the **standard deduction** for your filing status. **But** see page 31 if you checked any box on line 20a or 20b **OR** if someone can claim you as a dependent.
- Single—$4,250　● Married filing jointly or Qualifying widow(er)—$7,100
- Head of household—$6,250　● Married filing separately—$3,550　21　| 6,250 00 |

22 Subtract line 21 from line 19. If line 21 is more than line 19, enter -0-.　22　| 21,542 00 |

23 Multiply $2,700 by the total number of exemptions claimed on line 6d.　23　| 5,400 00 |

24 Subtract line 23 from line 22. If line 23 is more than line 22, enter -0-. This is your **taxable income.** ▶　24　| 16,142 00 |

Tax, credits, and payments

25 Find the tax on the amount on line 24 (see page 31).　25　| 2,419 00 |

26 Credit for child and dependent care expenses. Attach Schedule 2.　26　| 0 00 |

27 Credit for the elderly or the disabled. Attach Schedule 3.　27　| 0 00 |

28 Child tax credit (see page 32).　28　| 400 00 |

29 Education credits. Attach Form 8863.　29　| 0 00 |

30 Adoption credit. Attach Form 8839.　30　| 0 00 |

31 Add lines 26 through 30. These are your **total credits.**　31　| 400 00 |

32 Subtract line 31 from line 25. If line 31 is more than line 25, enter -0-.　32　| 2,019 00 |

33 Advance earned income credit payments from Form(s) W-2.　33　| 0 00 |

34 Add lines 32 and 33. This is your **total tax.** ▶　34　| 2,019 00 |

35 Total Federal income tax withheld from Forms W-2 and 1099.　35　| 3,094 00 |

36 1998 estimated tax payments and amount applied from 1997 return.　36　| 0 00 |

37a Earned income credit. Attach Schedule EIC if you have a qualifying child.　37a　| 0 00 |

b Nontaxable earned income: amount ▶ _____ and type ▶ _____

38 Additional child tax credit. Attach Form 8812.　38　| 0 00 |

39 Add lines 35, 36, 37a, and 38. These are your **total payments.** ▶　39　| 3,094 00 |

Refund

Have it directly deposited! See page 43 and fill in 41b, 41c, and 41d.

40 If line 39 is more than line 34, subtract line 34 from line 39. This is the amount you **overpaid.**　40　| 1,075 00 |

41a Amount of line 40 you want **refunded to you.**　41a　| 1,075 00 |

b Routing number ☐☐☐☐☐☐☐☐☐　**c** Type: ☐ Checking ☐ Savings

d Account number ☐☐☐☐☐☐☐☐☐☐☐☐☐☐☐☐☐

42 Amount of line 40 you want **applied to your 1999 estimated tax.**　42

Amount you owe

43 If line 34 is more than line 39, subtract line 39 from line 34. This is the **amount you owe.** For details on how to pay, see page 44.　43

44 Estimated tax penalty (see page 44).　44

Sign here

Joint return? See page 19. Keep a copy for your records.

Under penalties of perjury, I declare that I have examined this return and accompanying schedules and statements, and to the best of my knowledge and belief, they are true, correct, and accurately list all amounts and sources of income I received during the tax year. Declaration of preparer (other than the taxpayer) is based on all information of which the preparer has any knowledge.

Your signature ▶ _____ Date _____ Your occupation *Bookkeeper* Daytime telephone number (optional)

Spouse's signature. If joint return, BOTH must sign. _____ Date _____ Spouse's occupation _____ ( )

Paid preparer's use only

Preparer's signature ▶ _____ Date _____ Check if self-employed ☐ Preparer's social security no. _____

Firm's name (or yours if self-employed) and address ▶ _____ EIN _____ ZIP code _____

⊛

1040A FOR MARY WONG—CHILD TAX CREDIT WORKSHEET

Child Tax Credit Worksheet–Line 28

► Keep for your records.

Do Not File

1. $400.00 _____ I _____ . Multiply and enter the result . . . . 1. __400|00__
   ▲
   Enter number of qualifying children (see page 32)

2. Enter the amount from Form 1040A, line 19 . . . . . 2. __27,792|00__

3. Is line 2 above more than $55,000?

   ☒ **No.** Skip lines 3 through 5, enter -0- on line 6, and go to line 7.

   ☐ **Yes.** Enter: $75,000 if single, head of household, or qualifying widow(er); $110,000 if married filing jointly; $55,000 if married filing separately . . . . . 3. _____

4. Subtract line 3 from line 2. If zero or less, enter -0- here and on line 6, and go to line 7 . . . . 4. _____

5. Divide line 4 by $1,000. If the result is not a whole number, round it up to the next higher whole number (for example, round 0.01 to 1) . . . . 5. _____

6. Multiply $50 by the number on line 5 . . . . 6. __0|00__

7. Subtract line 6 from line 1. If zero or less, **stop here;** you **cannot** take this credit . 7. __400|00__

8. Enter the amount from Form 1040A, line 25 . . . . . 8. __2,419|00__

9. Is line 1 above more than $800?

   ☒ **No.** Add the amounts from Form 1040A, lines 26, 27, and 29. Enter the total.

   ☐ **Yes.** Enter the amount from the worksheet on page 34. } 9. __0|00__

10. Subtract line 9 above from line 8 . . . . 10. __2,419|00__

11. **Child tax credit.** Enter the **smaller** of line 7 or line 10 here and on Form 1040A, line 28 ► 11. __400|00__

TIP *If line 1 above is more than $800, you may be able to take the **Additional Child Tax Credit.** See page 32.*

COMPLETING THE 1040A—EXERCISE 3

ACTIVITY: Have students fill out the form for Ramon Flores.

Describe taxpayer

Ramon Flores is a dishwasher and a part-time janitor. He is not married but supports his two younger sisters with his salary. They do not live with him in the United States, but live in Guadalajara, Mexico.

He earned $11,600 from his first job and $5,500 from his second job. He has no savings account, and his deductions total $400. His employers withheld $1,200 from his pay.

Ramon has requested ITI numbers (by completing W-7 forms) for each of his sisters so that they may be included on his income tax return. Their numbers are:

Silvia Flores: 800-31-9906

Irma Flores: 800-92-7527

Ramon's Social Security number is 224-27-8103. He lives at 7184 Washington Avenue, Apt. C, Flint, Michigan 40000. He wants to contribute to the Presidential Election Campaign fund.

Ask Questions

1. Can Ramon use the 1040EZ instead of the 1040A?

   No. He wants to claim his sisters as dependents, and dependents cannot be listed on the 1040EZ.

2. Can Ramon file as head of household?

   No. His dependents do not live with him.

3. Is Ramon eligible for the earned income credit? (See the Appendix.)

   Ramon does not qualify for the credit because he does not have a child. See the Appendix.

1040A FOR RAMON FLORES—PAGE 1

Form	Department of the Treasury–Internal Revenue Service		
1040A	**U.S. Individual Income Tax Return**	**1998**	IRS Use Only–Do not write or staple in this space.

Label
(See page 18.)

Use the IRS label.

Otherwise, please print or type.

L A B E L   H E R E

Your first name and initial	Last name		
Ramon	Flores		

Your social security number
224 27 8103

If a joint return, spouse's first name and initial   Last name

Spouse's social security number

Home address (number and street). If you have a P.O. box, see page 19.   Apt. no.
7184 Washington Ave.   C

City, town or post office, state, and ZIP code. If you have a foreign address, see page 19.
Flint, MI 40000

OMB No. 1545-0085

▲ **IMPORTANT!** ▲
You **must** enter your SSN(s) above.

Presidential Election Campaign Fund (See page 19.)
Do you want $3 to go to this fund? . . . .   **Yes** [X] **No**
If a joint return, does your spouse want $3 to go to this fund?

Note: *Checking "Yes" will not change your tax or reduce your refund.*

Filing status

Check only one box.

1 [X] Single
2 [ ] Married filing joint return (even if only one had income)
3 [ ] Married filing separate return. Enter spouse's social security number above and full name here. ▶ _____
4 [ ] Head of household (with qualifying person). (See page 20.) If the qualifying person is a child but not your dependent, enter this child's name here. ▶ _____
5 [ ] Qualifying widow(er) with dependent child (year spouse died ▶ 19___). (See page 21.)

Exemptions

If more than seven dependents, see page 21.

6a [X] **Yourself.** If your parent (or someone else) can claim you as a dependent on his or her tax return, **do not** check box 6a.

b [ ] **Spouse**

c **Dependents:**

(1) First name Last name	(2) Dependent's social security number	(3) Dependent's relationship to you	(4) ✓ if qualified child for child tax credit (see page 22)
Silvia Flores	800 31 9906	sister	[ ]
Irma Flores	800 92 7527	sister	[ ]
			[ ]
			[ ]
			[ ]
			[ ]
			[ ]

No. of boxes checked on 6a and 6b **1**

No. of your children on 6c who:
• lived with you **0**
• did not live with you due to divorce or separation (see page 23) **0**

Dependents on 6c not entered above **2**

Add numbers entered on lines above **3**

d Total number of exemptions claimed.

Income

Attach Copy B of your Forms W-2 and 1099-R here.

If you did not get a W-2, see page 24.

Enclose, but do not staple, any payment.

7	Wages, salaries, tips, etc. Attach Form(s) W-2.	7	17,100 00
8a	**Taxable** interest. Attach Schedule 1 if required.	8a	0 00
b	**Tax-exempt** interest. DO NOT include on line 8a. 8b 0 00		
9	Ordinary dividends. Attach Schedule 1 if required.	9	0 00
10a	Total IRA distributions. 10a	10b Taxable amount (see page 24). 10b	0 00
11a	Total pensions and annuities. 11a	11b Taxable amount (see page 25). 11b	0 00
12	Unemployment compensation.	12	0 00
13a	Social security benefits. 13a	13b Taxable amount (see page 27). 13b	0 00
14	Add lines 7 through 13b (far right column). This is your **total income.** ▶	14	17,100 00

Adjusted gross income

15	IRA deduction (see page 28). 15 0 00		
16	Student loan interest deduction (see page 28). 16 0 00		
17	Add lines 15 and 16. These are your **total adjustments.**	17	0 00
18	Subtract line 17 from line 14. This is your **adjusted gross income.** If under $30,095 (under $10,030 if a child did not live with you), see the EIC instructions on page 36. ▶	18	17,100 00

For Disclosure, Privacy Act, and Paperwork Reduction Act Notice, see page 49.   Cat. No. 11327A   **1998** Form **1040A**

1040A FOR RAMON FLORES—PAGE 2

1998 Form 1040A page 2

Taxable income	**19**	Enter the amount from line 18.	**19**	17,100 00

20a Check if: ☐ **You** were 65 or older ☐ Blind **Enter number of boxes checked ▶** 20a ☐
☐ **Spouse** was 65 or older ☐ Blind

b If you are married filing separately and your spouse itemizes deductions, see page 30 and check here . . . . . . **▶** 20b ☐

21 Enter the **standard deduction** for your filing status. **But** see page 31 if you checked any box on line 20a or 20b **OR** if someone can claim you as a dependent.
- Single—$4,250 • Married filing jointly or Qualifying widow(er)—$7,100
- Head of household—$6,250 • Married filing separately—$3,550   **21** 4,250 00

22 Subtract line 21 from line 19. If line 21 is more than line 19, enter -0-. **22** 12,850 00

23 Multiply $2,700 by the total number of exemptions claimed on line 6d. **23** 8,100 00

24 Subtract line 23 from line 22. If line 23 is more than line 22, enter -0-. This is your **taxable income.** **▶ 24** 4,750 00

Tax, credits, and payments	**25**	Find the tax on the amount on line 24 (see page 31).	**25**	716 00

26 Credit for child and dependent care expenses. Attach Schedule 2. **26** 0 00

27 Credit for the elderly or the disabled. Attach Schedule 3. **27** 0 00

28 Child tax credit (see page 32). **28** 0 00

29 Education credits. Attach Form 8863. **29** 0 00

30 Adoption credit. Attach Form 8839. **30** 0 00

31 Add lines 26 through 30. These are your **total credits.** **31** 0 00

32 Subtract line 31 from line 25. If line 31 is more than line 25, enter -0-. **32** 716 00

33 Advance earned income credit payments from Form(s) W-2. **33** 0 00

34 Add lines 32 and 33. This is your **total tax.** **▶ 34** 716 00

35 Total Federal income tax withheld from Forms W-2 and 1099. **35** 1,200 00

36 1998 estimated tax payments and amount applied from 1997 return. **36** 0 00

37a Earned income credit. Attach Schedule EIC if you have a qualifying child. **37a** 0 00

b Nontaxable earned income: amount ▶   and type ▶

38 Additional child tax credit. Attach Form 8812. **38** 0 00

39 Add lines 35, 36, 37a, and 38. These are your **total payments.** **▶ 39** 1,200 00

Refund	**40**	If line 39 is more than line 34, subtract line 34 from line 39. This is the amount you **overpaid.**	**40**	484 00

Have it directly deposited! See page 43 and fill in 41b, 41c, and 41d.

41a Amount of line 40 you want **refunded to you.** **41a** 484 00

b Routing number ☐☐☐☐☐☐☐☐☐ **c** Type: ☐ Checking ☐ Savings

d Account number ☐☐☐☐☐☐☐☐☐☐☐☐☐☐☐☐☐

42 Amount of line 40 you want **applied to your 1999 estimated tax.** 42

Amount you owe	**43**	If line 34 is more than line 39, subtract line 39 from line 34. This is the **amount you owe.** For details on how to pay, see page 44.	**43**	
	44	Estimated tax penalty (see page 44). 44		

Sign here	Under penalties of perjury, I declare that I have examined this return and accompanying schedules and statements, and to the best of my knowledge and belief, they are true, correct, and accurately list all amounts and sources of income I received during the tax year. Declaration of preparer (other than the taxpayer) is based on all information of which the preparer has any knowledge.

Joint return? See page 19. Keep a copy for your records.

▶ Your signature   Date   Your occupation *Dishwasher/Janitor*   Daytime telephone number (optional)

Spouse's signature. If joint return, BOTH must sign.   Date   Spouse's occupation   (   )

Paid preparer's use only	Preparer's signature ▶ Date Check if self-employed ☐ Preparer's social security no.

Firm's name (or yours if self-employed) and address ▶   EIN
ZIP code

⊛

CHAPTER 8

Where to Get Help

OVERVIEW

Topics

Getting help from:

- IRS
- Books and libraries
- Tax preparers
- Phone book

Objectives

By the end of this chapter, the students will be able to:

- Identify several means of obtaining help with their tax questions and problems.

Student activities

- Complete a form with tax-help phone numbers and addresses for their region.

Things you need

- Local phone books.
- An example of Publication 17 and other IRS publications, if available.

Important points

- Ensure that students understand that they can get help and that they do not need to pay exorbitant fees for tax assistance, even if they pay for a professional tax preparer.

WHERE TO GET HELP

Describe chapter

In this chapter, you will learn about how you can get tax help from the following sources.

- **IRS**

    The IRS makes many rules that are often confusing, but the IRS also provides many kinds of free assistance to taxpayers.

- **Books and libraries**

    You can also get useful tax information from books and libraries.

- **Tax preparers**

    If you do not feel comfortable preparing your own tax return, or if you have a complex tax situation, you may wish to pay a professional tax preparer to complete your forms.

Before we go any further, let's discuss the vocabulary for this chapter.

VOCABULARY

ACTIVITY: Before providing the definitions, ask for volunteers to define each word. Write brief definitions on a transparency or on the blackboard, or send volunteers to the board to record their definitions, and have the class refine the sentence structure and spelling of each.

Have the students use each word in a sentence.

---

fee: Charge or payment.

assistor: Person who works for the IRS to help individuals with questions about their income tax forms.

attorney: Lawyer. Some lawyers specialize in tax law.

accountant: Person who prepares financial reports and gives financial advice. Many accountants prepare tax returns. An accountant with a special license from the state is called a CPA (certified public accountant).

ACTIVITY: Have students circle the first instance of each word in the chapter.

HELP FROM THE IRS

Describe help

The IRS wants all taxpayers to pay their taxes and file their tax return forms. For this reason, the IRS provides many ways to help taxpayers prepare their income tax return forms.

- **Publication 17**

  A tax guide for individuals, full of information on how to prepare your return and how to get more information.

  The publication is free, and you can order it by telephone or by mail.

- **Other IRS publications**

  Many IRS publications are available that provide detailed information on special topics.

  Some publications are available in Spanish.

- **Publications are free, and can be ordered from the IRS distribution center for your region.**

ACTIVITY: Show students Publication 17 or a list of available publications. Have them select two or three publications that they would like. Have them write down the name and/or number of the publication.

Discuss other help

In addition to publications, there are several other kinds of help you can get from the IRS.

- **The Internet:** www.irs@ustreas.gov

- **Tele-Tax**

  Recorded tax information on about 150 topics.

  Look in your phone book for the "Internal Revenue Service" in the U.S. Government Offices section for the phone number for your area, or consult Publication 17. The service is free.

- **VITA (Volunteer Income Tax Assistance) and TCE (Tax Counseling for the Elderly)**

  Free help for older, disabled, and non-English-speaking people.

  Call the IRS in your area to request the service.

- **Free tax help from the IRS**

  Order Publication 910 for a list of free publications and services available.

  Assistors are available at many local IRS offices. They can help you prepare your own return in a group setting. Call your local office for information.

  You may telephone the IRS for answers to questions about your return.

  You can send written questions to your IRS district director.

- **Forms by mail**

  You can request forms by mail by calling the IRS Forms Distribution Center in your region.

  The forms are free.

ACTIVITY: Ask students to call Tele-Tax and listen to a few topics. They could also write a short summary of what they heard.

LIBRARIES

Discuss libraries

Your local public library can provide you with a great deal of tax-related information. Beginning in late December, you can also get your forms at the library.

- **Forms**

    Commonly used forms, such as the 1040EZ and 1040A, are available in most libraries starting in December and January.

- **Videotaped instructions**

    Some libraries have videotaped instructions on how to fill out the tax return form.

- **Books**

    Libraries often have books with information on how to file your income tax. However, you must remember that the procedures change every year. You can use the books for general information, but be sure to look at the forms and instructions for current information.

    You can purchase books with current information from many bookstores. They are usually available in December and January. Many of these books are good if you need help with the long form, 1040, and if you itemize deductions.

ACTIVITY: Ask students to go to their library and find at least three tax resources. If the items can be checked out, the students can bring them to class to show the others.

TAX PREPARERS

Discuss tax preparers

Several types of tax preparers will fill out your income tax return form for you for a fee. These include:

- **Accountants**

    Some, but not all, are CPAs.

- **Professional tax preparers**

    Some people specialize in filling out tax returns. They are not necessarily accountants, but they are specially trained to fill out tax forms. They often advertise beginning in December and January.

    Be sure to compare services and prices of different tax preparers.

- **Tax attorneys**

    Some lawyers specialize in taxes, but it is not usually necessary to have an attorney fill out a tax form.

- **Tax preparation software**

    If you have a computer and a printer, there are a number of software programs that can help you complete your tax form.

    The advantage of these programs is that they perform the calculations for you.

You must remember that you are responsible for paying interest and penalties if you or your tax preparer makes a mistake.

ACTIVITY: If it is tax preparation season, have students look for advertisements for tax preparers and bring the ads to class. In class, have students compare services and fees.

TAX HELP—PHONE BOOK

ACTIVITY: Ask students to look in your phone book for the phone numbers and addresses of the organizations shown in the table in the workbook.

- IRS information is often found in the "U.S. Government Pages" of the phone book, at the beginning of the white pages, or in the white or business pages under "U.S. Government."

- The library information is often found in the city or county "Government Pages" of the phone book, at the beginning of the white pages, or under the name of the city or county in the white or business pages.

Ask

Do you have any questions about how you can get help with your tax questions and problems?

CONCLUSION

Review objectives

Now that you have completed this course, you are able to:

- Explain what federal income tax is.

- Explain your filing responsibilities and deadlines.

- Fill out the simple forms most people use.

- Obtain more information about federal income taxes.

Discuss yearly changes

Keep your student activity text for future reference, but remember that some of the rules and the amounts for exemptions, credits, and tax tables will change from year to year. Be sure to look at a current form for these amounts.

Now that you understand the basic concepts, it will be easier for you to work with the forms.

Tax Tables

1998 Tax Table

For persons with taxable incomes of less than $50,000

Example. Mr. and Mrs. Green are filing a joint return. Their taxable income on line 24 of Form 1040A is $23,250. First, they find the $23,250–23,300 income line. Next, they find the column for married filing jointly and read down the column. The amount shown where the income line and filing status column meet is $3,491. This is the tax amount they should enter on line 25 of Form 1040A.

At least	But less than	Single	Married filing jointly *	Married filing separately	Head of a house-hold
			Your tax is—		
23,200	23,250	3,484	3,484	3,750	3,484
23,250	23,300	3,491	(3,491)	3,764	3,491
23,300	23,350	3,499	3,499	3,778	3,499
23,350	23,400	3,506	3,506	3,792	3,506

If Form 1040A, line 24, is— At least	But less than	Single	Married filing jointly *	Married filing separately	Head of a house-hold
			Your tax is—		
$0	$5	$0	$0	$0	$0
5	15	2	2	2	2
15	25	3	3	3	3
25	50	6	6	6	6
50	75	9	9	9	9
75	100	13	13	13	13
100	125	17	17	17	17
125	150	21	21	21	21
150	175	24	24	24	24
175	200	28	28	28	28
200	225	32	32	32	32
225	250	36	36	36	36
250	275	39	39	39	39
275	300	43	43	43	43
300	325	47	47	47	47
325	350	51	51	51	51
350	375	54	54	54	54
375	400	58	58	58	58
400	425	62	62	62	62
425	450	66	66	66	66
450	475	69	69	69	69
475	500	73	73	73	73
500	525	77	77	77	77
525	550	81	81	81	81
550	575	84	84	84	84
575	600	88	88	88	88
600	625	92	92	92	92
625	650	96	96	96	96
650	675	99	99	99	99
675	700	103	103	103	103
700	725	107	107	107	107
725	750	111	111	111	111
750	775	114	114	114	114
775	800	118	118	118	118
800	825	122	122	122	122
825	850	126	126	126	126
850	875	129	129	129	129
875	900	133	133	133	133
900	925	137	137	137	137
925	950	141	141	141	141
950	975	144	144	144	144
975	1,000	148	148	148	148
1,000					
1,000	1,025	152	152	152	152
1,025	1,050	156	156	156	156
1,050	1,075	159	159	159	159
1,075	1,100	163	163	163	163
1,100	1,125	167	167	167	167
1,125	1,150	171	171	171	171
1,150	1,175	174	174	174	174
1,175	1,200	178	178	178	178
1,200	1,225	182	182	182	182
1,225	1,250	186	186	186	186
1,250	1,275	189	189	189	189
1,275	1,300	193	193	193	193

If Form 1040A, line 24, is— At least	But less than	Single	Married filing jointly *	Married filing separately	Head of a house-hold
			Your tax is—		
1,300	1,325	197	197	197	197
1,325	1,350	201	201	201	201
1,350	1,375	204	204	204	204
1,375	1,400	208	208	208	208
1,400	1,425	212	212	212	212
1,425	1,450	216	216	216	216
1,450	1,475	219	219	219	219
1,475	1,500	223	223	223	223
1,500	1,525	227	227	227	227
1,525	1,550	231	231	231	231
1,550	1,575	234	234	234	234
1,575	1,600	238	238	238	238
1,600	1,625	242	242	242	242
1,625	1,650	246	246	246	246
1,650	1,675	249	249	249	249
1,675	1,700	253	253	253	253
1,700	1,725	257	257	257	257
1,725	1,750	261	261	261	261
1,750	1,775	264	264	264	264
1,775	1,800	268	268	268	268
1,800	1,825	272	272	272	272
1,825	1,850	276	276	276	276
1,850	1,875	279	279	279	279
1,875	1,900	283	283	283	283
1,900	1,925	287	287	287	287
1,925	1,950	291	291	291	291
1,950	1,975	294	294	294	294
1,975	2,000	298	298	298	298
2,000					
2,000	2,025	302	302	302	302
2,025	2,050	306	306	306	306
2,050	2,075	309	309	309	309
2,075	2,100	313	313	313	313
2,100	2,125	317	317	317	317
2,125	2,150	321	321	321	321
2,150	2,175	324	324	324	324
2,175	2,200	328	328	328	328
2,200	2,225	332	332	332	332
2,225	2,250	336	336	336	336
2,250	2,275	339	339	339	339
2,275	2,300	343	343	343	343
2,300	2,325	347	347	347	347
2,325	2,350	351	351	351	351
2,350	2,375	354	354	354	354
2,375	2,400	358	358	358	358
2,400	2,425	362	362	362	362
2,425	2,450	366	366	366	366
2,450	2,475	369	369	369	369
2,475	2,500	373	373	373	373
2,500	2,525	377	377	377	377
2,525	2,550	381	381	381	381
2,550	2,575	384	384	384	384
2,575	2,600	388	388	388	388
2,600	2,625	392	392	392	392
2,625	2,650	396	396	396	396
2,650	2,675	399	399	399	399
2,675	2,700	403	403	403	403

If Form 1040A, line 24, is— At least	But less than	Single	Married filing jointly *	Married filing separately	Head of a house-hold
			Your tax is—		
2,700	2,725	407	407	407	407
2,725	2,750	411	411	411	411
2,750	2,775	414	414	414	414
2,775	2,800	418	418	418	418
2,800	2,825	422	422	422	422
2,825	2,850	426	426	426	426
2,850	2,875	429	429	429	429
2,875	2,900	433	433	433	433
2,900	2,925	437	437	437	437
2,925	2,950	441	441	441	441
2,950	2,975	444	444	444	444
2,975	3,000	448	448	448	448
3,000					
3,000	3,050	454	454	454	454
3,050	3,100	461	461	461	461
3,100	3,150	469	469	469	469
3,150	3,200	476	476	476	476
3,200	3,250	484	484	484	484
3,250	3,300	491	491	491	491
3,300	3,350	499	499	499	499
3,350	3,400	506	506	506	506
3,400	3,450	514	514	514	514
3,450	3,500	521	521	521	521
3,500	3,550	529	529	529	529
3,550	3,600	536	536	536	536
3,600	3,650	544	544	544	544
3,650	3,700	551	551	551	551
3,700	3,750	559	559	559	559
3,750	3,800	566	566	566	566
3,800	3,850	574	574	574	574
3,850	3,900	581	581	581	581
3,900	3,950	589	589	589	589
3,950	4,000	596	596	596	596
4,000					
4,000	4,050	604	604	604	604
4,050	4,100	611	611	611	611
4,100	4,150	619	619	619	619
4,150	4,200	626	626	626	626
4,200	4,250	634	634	634	634
4,250	4,300	641	641	641	641
4,300	4,350	649	649	649	649
4,350	4,400	656	656	656	656
4,400	4,450	664	664	664	664
4,450	4,500	671	671	671	671
4,500	4,550	679	679	679	679
4,550	4,600	686	686	686	686
4,600	4,650	694	694	694	694
4,650	4,700	701	701	701	701
4,700	4,750	709	709	709	709
4,750	4,800	716	716	716	716
4,800	4,850	724	724	724	724
4,850	4,900	731	731	731	731
4,900	4,950	739	739	739	739
4,950	5,000	746	746	746	746

Continued on next page

* This column must also be used by a qualifying widow(er).

1998 Tax Table—*Continued*

If Form 1040A, line 24, is—		And you are—				If Form 1040A, line 24, is—		And you are—				If Form 1040A, line 24, is—		And you are—			
At least	But less than	Single	Married filing jointly *	Married filing sepa-rately	Head of a house-hold	At least	But less than	Single	Married filing jointly *	Married filing sepa-rately	Head of a house-hold	At least	But less than	Single	Married filing jointly *	Married filing sepa-rately	Head of a house-hold
		Your tax is—						Your tax is—						Your tax is—			
5,000						**8,000**						**11,000**					
5,000	5,050	754	754	754	754	8,000	8,050	1,204	1,204	1,204	1,204	11,000	11,050	1,654	1,654	1,654	1,654
5,050	5,100	761	761	761	761	8,050	8,100	1,211	1,211	1,211	1,211	11,050	11,100	1,661	1,661	1,661	1,661
5,100	5,150	769	769	769	769	8,100	8,150	1,219	1,219	1,219	1,219	11,100	11,150	1,669	1,669	1,669	1,669
5,150	5,200	776	776	776	776	8,150	8,200	1,226	1,226	1,226	1,226	11,150	11,200	1,676	1,676	1,676	1,676
5,200	5,250	784	784	784	784	8,200	8,250	1,234	1,234	1,234	1,234	11,200	11,250	1,684	1,684	1,684	1,684
5,250	5,300	791	791	791	791	8,250	8,300	1,241	1,241	1,241	1,241	11,250	11,300	1,691	1,691	1,691	1,691
5,300	5,350	799	799	799	799	8,300	8,350	1,249	1,249	1,249	1,249	11,300	11,350	1,699	1,699	1,699	1,699
5,350	5,400	806	806	806	806	8,350	8,400	1,256	1,256	1,256	1,256	11,350	11,400	1,706	1,706	1,706	1,706
5,400	5,450	814	814	814	814	8,400	8,450	1,264	1,264	1,264	1,264	11,400	11,450	1,714	1,714	1,714	1,714
5,450	5,500	821	821	821	821	8,450	8,500	1,271	1,271	1,271	1,271	11,450	11,500	1,721	1,721	1,721	1,721
5,500	5,550	829	829	829	829	8,500	8,550	1,279	1,279	1,279	1,279	11,500	11,550	1,729	1,729	1,729	1,729
5,550	5,600	836	836	836	836	8,550	8,600	1,286	1,286	1,286	1,286	11,550	11,600	1,736	1,736	1,736	1,736
5,600	5,650	844	844	844	844	8,600	8,650	1,294	1,294	1,294	1,294	11,600	11,650	1,744	1,744	1,744	1,744
5,650	5,700	851	851	851	851	8,650	8,700	1,301	1,301	1,301	1,301	11,650	11,700	1,751	1,751	1,751	1,751
5,700	5,750	859	859	859	859	8,700	8,750	1,309	1,309	1,309	1,309	11,700	11,750	1,759	1,759	1,759	1,759
5,750	5,800	866	866	866	866	8,750	8,800	1,316	1,316	1,316	1,316	11,750	11,800	1,766	1,766	1,766	1,766
5,800	5,850	874	874	874	874	8,800	8,850	1,324	1,324	1,324	1,324	11,800	11,850	1,774	1,774	1,774	1,774
5,850	5,900	881	881	881	881	8,850	8,900	1,331	1,331	1,331	1,331	11,850	11,900	1,781	1,781	1,781	1,781
5,900	5,950	889	889	889	889	8,900	8,950	1,339	1,339	1,339	1,339	11,900	11,950	1,789	1,789	1,789	1,789
5,950	6,000	896	896	896	896	8,950	9,000	1,346	1,346	1,346	1,346	11,950	12,000	1,796	1,796	1,796	1,796
6,000						**9,000**						**12,000**					
6,000	6,050	904	904	904	904	9,000	9,050	1,354	1,354	1,354	1,354	12,000	12,050	1,804	1,804	1,804	1,804
6,050	6,100	911	911	911	911	9,050	9,100	1,361	1,361	1,361	1,361	12,050	12,100	1,811	1,811	1,811	1,811
6,100	6,150	919	919	919	919	9,100	9,150	1,369	1,369	1,369	1,369	12,100	12,150	1,819	1,819	1,819	1,819
6,150	6,200	926	926	926	926	9,150	9,200	1,376	1,376	1,376	1,376	12,150	12,200	1,826	1,826	1,826	1,826
6,200	6,250	934	934	934	934	9,200	9,250	1,384	1,384	1,384	1,384	12,200	12,250	1,834	1,834	1,834	1,834
6,250	6,300	941	941	941	941	9,250	9,300	1,391	1,391	1,391	1,391	12,250	12,300	1,841	1,841	1,841	1,841
6,300	6,350	949	949	949	949	9,300	9,350	1,399	1,399	1,399	1,399	12,300	12,350	1,849	1,849	1,849	1,849
6,350	6,400	956	956	956	956	9,350	9,400	1,406	1,406	1,406	1,406	12,350	12,400	1,856	1,856	1,856	1,856
6,400	6,450	964	964	964	964	9,400	9,450	1,414	1,414	1,414	1,414	12,400	12,450	1,864	1,864	1,864	1,864
6,450	6,500	971	971	971	971	9,450	9,500	1,421	1,421	1,421	1,421	12,450	12,500	1,871	1,871	1,871	1,871
6,500	6,550	979	979	979	979	9,500	9,550	1,429	1,429	1,429	1,429	12,500	12,550	1,879	1,879	1,879	1,879
6,550	6,600	986	986	986	986	9,550	9,600	1,436	1,436	1,436	1,436	12,550	12,600	1,886	1,886	1,886	1,886
6,600	6,650	994	994	994	994	9,600	9,650	1,444	1,444	1,444	1,444	12,600	12,650	1,894	1,894	1,894	1,894
6,650	6,700	1,001	1,001	1,001	1,001	9,650	9,700	1,451	1,451	1,451	1,451	12,650	12,700	1,901	1,901	1,901	1,901
6,700	6,750	1,009	1,009	1,009	1,009	9,700	9,750	1,459	1,459	1,459	1,459	12,700	12,750	1,909	1,909	1,909	1,909
6,750	6,800	1,016	1,016	1,016	1,016	9,750	9,800	1,466	1,466	1,466	1,466	12,750	12,800	1,916	1,916	1,916	1,916
6,800	6,850	1,024	1,024	1,024	1,024	9,800	9,850	1,474	1,474	1,474	1,474	12,800	12,850	1,924	1,924	1,924	1,924
6,850	6,900	1,031	1,031	1,031	1,031	9,850	9,900	1,481	1,481	1,481	1,481	12,850	12,900	1,931	1,931	1,931	1,931
6,900	6,950	1,039	1,039	1,039	1,039	9,900	9,950	1,489	1,489	1,489	1,489	12,900	12,950	1,939	1,939	1,939	1,939
6,950	7,000	1,046	1,046	1,046	1,046	9,950	10,000	1,496	1,496	1,496	1,496	12,950	13,000	1,946	1,946	1,946	1,946
7,000						**10,000**						**13,000**					
7,000	7,050	1,054	1,054	1,054	1,054	10,000	10,050	1,504	1,504	1,504	1,504	13,000	13,050	1,954	1,954	1,954	1,954
7,050	7,100	1,061	1,061	1,061	1,061	10,050	10,100	1,511	1,511	1,511	1,511	13,050	13,100	1,961	1,961	1,961	1,961
7,100	7,150	1,069	1,069	1,069	1,069	10,100	10,150	1,519	1,519	1,519	1,519	13,100	13,150	1,969	1,969	1,969	1,969
7,150	7,200	1,076	1,076	1,076	1,076	10,150	10,200	1,526	1,526	1,526	1,526	13,150	13,200	1,976	1,976	1,976	1,976
7,200	7,250	1,084	1,084	1,084	1,084	10,200	10,250	1,534	1,534	1,534	1,534	13,200	13,250	1,984	1,984	1,984	1,984
7,250	7,300	1,091	1,091	1,091	1,091	10,250	10,300	1,541	1,541	1,541	1,541	13,250	13,300	1,991	1,991	1,991	1,991
7,300	7,350	1,099	1,099	1,099	1,099	10,300	10,350	1,549	1,549	1,549	1,549	13,300	13,350	1,999	1,999	1,999	1,999
7,350	7,400	1,106	1,106	1,106	1,106	10,350	10,400	1,556	1,556	1,556	1,556	13,350	13,400	2,006	2,006	2,006	2,006
7,400	7,450	1,114	1,114	1,114	1,114	10,400	10,450	1,564	1,564	1,564	1,564	13,400	13,450	2,014	2,014	2,014	2,014
7,450	7,500	1,121	1,121	1,121	1,121	10,450	10,500	1,571	1,571	1,571	1,571	13,450	13,500	2,021	2,021	2,021	2,021
7,500	7,550	1,129	1,129	1,129	1,129	10,500	10,550	1,579	1,579	1,579	1,579	13,500	13,550	2,029	2,029	2,029	2,029
7,550	7,600	1,136	1,136	1,136	1,136	10,550	10,600	1,586	1,586	1,586	1,586	13,550	13,600	2,036	2,036	2,036	2,036
7,600	7,650	1,144	1,144	1,144	1,144	10,600	10,650	1,594	1,594	1,594	1,594	13,600	13,650	2,044	2,044	2,044	2,044
7,650	7,700	1,151	1,151	1,151	1,151	10,650	10,700	1,601	1,601	1,601	1,601	13,650	13,700	2,051	2,051	2,051	2,051
7,700	7,750	1,159	1,159	1,159	1,159	10,700	10,750	1,609	1,609	1,609	1,609	13,700	13,750	2,059	2,059	2,059	2,059
7,750	7,800	1,166	1,166	1,166	1,166	10,750	10,800	1,616	1,616	1,616	1,616	13,750	13,800	2,066	2,066	2,066	2,066
7,800	7,850	1,174	1,174	1,174	1,174	10,800	10,850	1,624	1,624	1,624	1,624	13,800	13,850	2,074	2,074	2,074	2,074
7,850	7,900	1,181	1,181	1,181	1,181	10,850	10,900	1,631	1,631	1,631	1,631	13,850	13,900	2,081	2,081	2,081	2,081
7,900	7,950	1,189	1,189	1,189	1,189	10,900	10,950	1,639	1,639	1,639	1,639	13,900	13,950	2,089	2,089	2,089	2,089
7,950	8,000	1,196	1,196	1,196	1,196	10,950	11,000	1,646	1,646	1,646	1,646	13,950	14,000	2,096	2,096	2,096	2,096

* This column must also be used by a qualifying widow(er).

Continued on next page

1998 Tax Table—*Continued*

If Form 1040A, line 24, is—		And you are—			
At least	But less than	Single	Married filing jointly *	Married filing separately	Head of a household
		Your tax is—			
14,000					
14,000	14,050	2,104	2,104	2,104	2,104
14,050	14,100	2,111	2,111	2,111	2,111
14,100	14,150	2,119	2,119	2,119	2,119
14,150	14,200	2,126	2,126	2,126	2,126
14,200	14,250	2,134	2,134	2,134	2,134
14,250	14,300	2,141	2,141	2,141	2,141
14,300	14,350	2,149	2,149	2,149	2,149
14,350	14,400	2,156	2,156	2,156	2,156
14,400	14,450	2,164	2,164	2,164	2,164
14,450	14,500	2,171	2,171	2,171	2,171
14,500	14,550	2,179	2,179	2,179	2,179
14,550	14,600	2,186	2,186	2,186	2,186
14,600	14,650	2,194	2,194	2,194	2,194
14,650	14,700	2,201	2,201	2,201	2,201
14,700	14,750	2,209	2,209	2,209	2,209
14,750	14,800	2,216	2,216	2,216	2,216
14,800	14,850	2,224	2,224	2,224	2,224
14,850	14,900	2,231	2,231	2,231	2,231
14,900	14,950	2,239	2,239	2,239	2,239
14,950	15,000	2,246	2,246	2,246	2,246
15,000					
15,000	15,050	2,254	2,254	2,254	2,254
15,050	15,100	2,261	2,261	2,261	2,261
15,100	15,150	2,269	2,269	2,269	2,269
15,150	15,200	2,276	2,276	2,276	2,276
15,200	15,250	2,284	2,284	2,284	2,284
15,250	15,300	2,291	2,291	2,291	2,291
15,300	15,350	2,299	2,299	2,299	2,299
15,350	15,400	2,306	2,306	2,306	2,306
15,400	15,450	2,314	2,314	2,314	2,314
15,450	15,500	2,321	2,321	2,321	2,321
15,500	15,550	2,329	2,329	2,329	2,329
15,550	15,600	2,336	2,336	2,336	2,336
15,600	15,650	2,344	2,344	2,344	2,344
15,650	15,700	2,351	2,351	2,351	2,351
15,700	15,750	2,359	2,359	2,359	2,359
15,750	15,800	2,366	2,366	2,366	2,366
15,800	15,850	2,374	2,374	2,374	2,374
15,850	15,900	2,381	2,381	2,381	2,381
15,900	15,950	2,389	2,389	2,389	2,389
15,950	16,000	2,396	2,396	2,396	2,396
16,000					
16,000	16,050	2,404	2,404	2,404	2,404
16,050	16,100	2,411	2,411	2,411	2,411
16,100	16,150	2,419	2,419	2,419	2,419
16,150	16,200	2,426	2,426	2,426	2,426
16,200	16,250	2,434	2,434	2,434	2,434
16,250	16,300	2,441	2,441	2,441	2,441
16,300	16,350	2,449	2,449	2,449	2,449
16,350	16,400	2,456	2,456	2,456	2,456
16,400	16,450	2,464	2,464	2,464	2,464
16,450	16,500	2,471	2,471	2,471	2,471
16,500	16,550	2,479	2,479	2,479	2,479
16,550	16,600	2,486	2,486	2,486	2,486
16,600	16,650	2,494	2,494	2,494	2,494
16,650	16,700	2,501	2,501	2,501	2,501
16,700	16,750	2,509	2,509	2,509	2,509
16,750	16,800	2,516	2,516	2,516	2,516
16,800	16,850	2,524	2,524	2,524	2,524
16,850	16,900	2,531	2,531	2,531	2,531
16,900	16,950	2,539	2,539	2,539	2,539
16,950	17,000	2,546	2,546	2,546	2,546

If Form 1040A, line 24, is—		And you are—			
At least	But less than	Single	Married filing jointly *	Married filing separately	Head of a household
		Your tax is—			
17,000					
17,000	17,050	2,554	2,554	2,554	2,554
17,050	17,100	2,561	2,561	2,561	2,561
17,100	17,150	2,569	2,569	2,569	2,569
17,150	17,200	2,576	2,576	2,576	2,576
17,200	17,250	2,584	2,584	2,584	2,584
17,250	17,300	2,591	2,591	2,591	2,591
17,300	17,350	2,599	2,599	2,599	2,599
17,350	17,400	2,606	2,606	2,606	2,606
17,400	17,450	2,614	2,614	2,614	2,614
17,450	17,500	2,621	2,621	2,621	2,621
17,500	17,550	2,629	2,629	2,629	2,629
17,550	17,600	2,636	2,636	2,636	2,636
17,600	17,650	2,644	2,644	2,644	2,644
17,650	17,700	2,651	2,651	2,651	2,651
17,700	17,750	2,659	2,659	2,659	2,659
17,750	17,800	2,666	2,666	2,666	2,666
17,800	17,850	2,674	2,674	2,674	2,674
17,850	17,900	2,681	2,681	2,681	2,681
17,900	17,950	2,689	2,689	2,689	2,689
17,950	18,000	2,696	2,696	2,696	2,696
18,000					
18,000	18,050	2,704	2,704	2,704	2,704
18,050	18,100	2,711	2,711	2,711	2,711
18,100	18,150	2,719	2,719	2,719	2,719
18,150	18,200	2,726	2,726	2,726	2,726
18,200	18,250	2,734	2,734	2,734	2,734
18,250	18,300	2,741	2,741	2,741	2,741
18,300	18,350	2,749	2,749	2,749	2,749
18,350	18,400	2,756	2,756	2,756	2,756
18,400	18,450	2,764	2,764	2,764	2,764
18,450	18,500	2,771	2,771	2,771	2,771
18,500	18,550	2,779	2,779	2,779	2,779
18,550	18,600	2,786	2,786	2,786	2,786
18,600	18,650	2,794	2,794	2,794	2,794
18,650	18,700	2,801	2,801	2,801	2,801
18,700	18,750	2,809	2,809	2,809	2,809
18,750	18,800	2,816	2,816	2,816	2,816
18,800	18,850	2,824	2,824	2,824	2,824
18,850	18,900	2,831	2,831	2,831	2,831
18,900	18,950	2,839	2,839	2,839	2,839
18,950	19,000	2,846	2,846	2,846	2,846
19,000					
19,000	19,050	2,854	2,854	2,854	2,854
19,050	19,100	2,861	2,861	2,861	2,861
19,100	19,150	2,869	2,869	2,869	2,869
19,150	19,200	2,876	2,876	2,876	2,876
19,200	19,250	2,884	2,884	2,884	2,884
19,250	19,300	2,891	2,891	2,891	2,891
19,300	19,350	2,899	2,899	2,899	2,899
19,350	19,400	2,906	2,906	2,906	2,906
19,400	19,450	2,914	2,914	2,914	2,914
19,450	19,500	2,921	2,921	2,921	2,921
19,500	19,550	2,929	2,929	2,929	2,929
19,550	19,600	2,936	2,936	2,936	2,936
19,600	19,650	2,944	2,944	2,944	2,944
19,650	19,700	2,951	2,951	2,951	2,951
19,700	19,750	2,959	2,959	2,959	2,959
19,750	19,800	2,966	2,966	2,966	2,966
19,800	19,850	2,974	2,974	2,974	2,974
19,850	19,900	2,981	2,981	2,981	2,981
19,900	19,950	2,989	2,989	2,989	2,989
19,950	20,000	2,996	2,996	2,996	2,996

If Form 1040A, line 24, is—		And you are—			
At least	But less than	Single	Married filing jointly *	Married filing separately	Head of a household
		Your tax is—			
20,000					
20,000	20,050	3,004	3,004	3,004	3,004
20,050	20,100	3,011	3,011	3,011	3,011
20,100	20,150	3,019	3,019	3,019	3,019
20,150	20,200	3,026	3,026	3,026	3,026
20,200	20,250	3,034	3,034	3,034	3,034
20,250	20,300	3,041	3,041	3,041	3,041
20,300	20,350	3,049	3,049	3,049	3,049
20,350	20,400	3,056	3,056	3,056	3,056
20,400	20,450	3,064	3,064	3,064	3,064
20,450	20,500	3,071	3,071	3,071	3,071
20,500	20,550	3,079	3,079	3,079	3,079
20,550	20,600	3,086	3,086	3,086	3,086
20,600	20,650	3,094	3,094	3,094	3,094
20,650	20,700	3,101	3,101	3,101	3,101
20,700	20,750	3,109	3,109	3,109	3,109
20,750	20,800	3,116	3,116	3,116	3,116
20,800	20,850	3,124	3,124	3,124	3,124
20,850	20,900	3,131	3,131	3,131	3,131
20,900	20,950	3,139	3,139	3,139	3,139
20,950	21,000	3,146	3,146	3,146	3,146
21,000					
21,000	21,050	3,154	3,154	3,154	3,154
21,050	21,100	3,161	3,161	3,161	3,161
21,100	21,150	3,169	3,169	3,169	3,169
21,150	21,200	3,176	3,176	3,176	3,176
21,200	21,250	3,184	3,184	3,190	3,184
21,250	21,300	3,191	3,191	3,204	3,191
21,300	21,350	3,199	3,199	3,218	3,199
21,350	21,400	3,206	3,206	3,232	3,206
21,400	21,450	3,214	3,214	3,246	3,214
21,450	21,500	3,221	3,221	3,260	3,221
21,500	21,550	3,229	3,229	3,274	3,229
21,550	21,600	3,236	3,236	3,288	3,236
21,600	21,650	3,244	3,244	3,302	3,244
21,650	21,700	3,251	3,251	3,316	3,251
21,700	21,750	3,259	3,259	3,330	3,259
21,750	21,800	3,266	3,266	3,344	3,266
21,800	21,850	3,274	3,274	3,358	3,274
21,850	21,900	3,281	3,281	3,372	3,281
21,900	21,950	3,289	3,289	3,386	3,289
21,950	22,000	3,296	3,296	3,400	3,296
22,000					
22,000	22,050	3,304	3,304	3,414	3,304
22,050	22,100	3,311	3,311	3,428	3,311
22,100	22,150	3,319	3,319	3,442	3,319
22,150	22,200	3,326	3,326	3,456	3,326
22,200	22,250	3,334	3,334	3,470	3,334
22,250	22,300	3,341	3,341	3,484	3,341
22,300	22,350	3,349	3,349	3,498	3,349
22,350	22,400	3,356	3,356	3,512	3,356
22,400	22,450	3,364	3,364	3,526	3,364
22,450	22,500	3,371	3,371	3,540	3,371
22,500	22,550	3,379	3,379	3,554	3,379
22,550	22,600	3,386	3,386	3,568	3,386
22,600	22,650	3,394	3,394	3,582	3,394
22,650	22,700	3,401	3,401	3,596	3,401
22,700	22,750	3,409	3,409	3,610	3,409
22,750	22,800	3,416	3,416	3,624	3,416
22,800	22,850	3,424	3,424	3,638	3,424
22,850	22,900	3,431	3,431	3,652	3,431
22,900	22,950	3,439	3,439	3,666	3,439
22,950	23,000	3,446	3,446	3,680	3,446

* This column must also be used by a qualifying widow(er).

Continued on next page

1998 Tax Table—*Continued*

If Form 1040A, line 24, is— At least	But less than	And you are— Single	Married filing jointly *	Married filing separately	Head of a household
		Your tax is—			
23,000					
23,000	**23,050**	3,454	3,454	3,694	3,454
23,050	**23,100**	3,461	3,461	3,708	3,461
23,100	**23,150**	3,469	3,469	3,722	3,469
23,150	**23,200**	3,476	3,476	3,736	3,476
23,200	**23,250**	3,484	3,484	3,750	3,484
23,250	**23,300**	3,491	3,491	3,764	3,491
23,300	**23,350**	3,499	3,499	3,778	3,499
23,350	**23,400**	3,506	3,506	3,792	3,506
23,400	**23,450**	3,514	3,514	3,806	3,514
23,450	**23,500**	3,521	3,521	3,820	3,521
23,500	**23,550**	3,529	3,529	3,834	3,529
23,550	**23,600**	3,536	3,536	3,848	3,536
23,600	**23,650**	3,544	3,544	3,862	3,544
23,650	**23,700**	3,551	3,551	3,876	3,551
23,700	**23,750**	3,559	3,559	3,890	3,559
23,750	**23,800**	3,566	3,566	3,904	3,566
23,800	**23,850**	3,574	3,574	3,918	3,574
23,850	**23,900**	3,581	3,581	3,932	3,581
23,900	**23,950**	3,589	3,589	3,946	3,589
23,950	**24,000**	3,596	3,596	3,960	3,596
24,000					
24,000	**24,050**	3,604	3,604	3,974	3,604
24,050	**24,100**	3,611	3,611	3,988	3,611
24,100	**24,150**	3,619	3,619	4,002	3,619
24,150	**24,200**	3,626	3,626	4,016	3,626
24,200	**24,250**	3,634	3,634	4,030	3,634
24,250	**24,300**	3,641	3,641	4,044	3,641
24,300	**24,350**	3,649	3,649	4,058	3,649
24,350	**24,400**	3,656	3,656	4,072	3,656
24,400	**24,450**	3,664	3,664	4,086	3,664
24,450	**24,500**	3,671	3,671	4,100	3,671
24,500	**24,550**	3,679	3,679	4,114	3,679
24,550	**24,600**	3,686	3,686	4,128	3,686
24,600	**24,650**	3,694	3,694	4,142	3,694
24,650	**24,700**	3,701	3,701	4,156	3,701
24,700	**24,750**	3,709	3,709	4,170	3,709
24,750	**24,800**	3,716	3,716	4,184	3,716
24,800	**24,850**	3,724	3,724	4,198	3,724
24,850	**24,900**	3,731	3,731	4,212	3,731
24,900	**24,950**	3,739	3,739	4,226	3,739
24,950	**25,000**	3,746	3,746	4,240	3,746
25,000					
25,000	**25,050**	3,754	3,754	4,254	3,754
25,050	**25,100**	3,761	3,761	4,268	3,761
25,100	**25,150**	3,769	3,769	4,282	3,769
25,150	**25,200**	3,776	3,776	4,296	3,776
25,200	**25,250**	3,784	3,784	4,310	3,784
25,250	**25,300**	3,791	3,791	4,324	3,791
25,300	**25,350**	3,799	3,799	4,338	3,799
25,350	**25,400**	3,810	3,806	4,352	3,806
25,400	**25,450**	3,824	3,814	4,366	3,814
25,450	**25,500**	3,838	3,821	4,380	3,821
25,500	**25,550**	3,852	3,829	4,394	3,829
25,550	**25,600**	3,866	3,836	4,408	3,836
25,600	**25,650**	3,880	3,844	4,422	3,844
25,650	**25,700**	3,894	3,851	4,436	3,851
25,700	**25,750**	3,908	3,859	4,450	3,859
25,750	**25,800**	3,922	3,866	4,464	3,866
25,800	**25,850**	3,936	3,874	4,478	3,874
25,850	**25,900**	3,950	3,881	4,492	3,881
25,900	**25,950**	3,964	3,889	4,506	3,889
25,950	**26,000**	3,978	3,896	4,520	3,896

If Form 1040A, line 24, is— At least	But less than	And you are— Single	Married filing jointly *	Married filing separately	Head of a household
		Your tax is—			
26,000					
26,000	**26,050**	3,992	3,904	4,534	3,904
26,050	**26,100**	4,006	3,911	4,548	3,911
26,100	**26,150**	4,020	3,919	4,562	3,919
26,150	**26,200**	4,034	3,926	4,576	3,926
26,200	**26,250**	4,048	3,934	4,590	3,934
26,250	**26,300**	4,062	3,941	4,604	3,941
26,300	**26,350**	4,076	3,949	4,618	3,949
26,350	**26,400**	4,090	3,956	4,632	3,956
26,400	**26,450**	4,104	3,964	4,646	3,964
26,450	**26,500**	4,118	3,971	4,660	3,971
26,500	**26,550**	4,132	3,979	4,674	3,979
26,550	**26,600**	4,146	3,986	4,688	3,986
26,600	**26,650**	4,160	3,994	4,702	3,994
26,650	**26,700**	4,174	4,001	4,716	4,001
26,700	**26,750**	4,188	4,009	4,730	4,009
26,750	**26,800**	4,202	4,016	4,744	4,016
26,800	**26,850**	4,216	4,024	4,758	4,024
26,850	**26,900**	4,230	4,031	4,772	4,031
26,900	**26,950**	4,244	4,039	4,786	4,039
26,950	**27,000**	4,258	4,046	4,800	4,046
27,000					
27,000	**27,050**	4,272	4,054	4,814	4,054
27,050	**27,100**	4,286	4,061	4,828	4,061
27,100	**27,150**	4,300	4,069	4,842	4,069
27,150	**27,200**	4,314	4,076	4,856	4,076
27,200	**27,250**	4,328	4,084	4,870	4,084
27,250	**27,300**	4,342	4,091	4,884	4,091
27,300	**27,350**	4,356	4,099	4,898	4,099
27,350	**27,400**	4,370	4,106	4,912	4,106
27,400	**27,450**	4,384	4,114	4,926	4,114
27,450	**27,500**	4,398	4,121	4,940	4,121
27,500	**27,550**	4,412	4,129	4,954	4,129
27,550	**27,600**	4,426	4,136	4,968	4,136
27,600	**27,650**	4,440	4,144	4,982	4,144
27,650	**27,700**	4,454	4,151	4,996	4,151
27,700	**27,750**	4,468	4,159	5,010	4,159
27,750	**27,800**	4,482	4,166	5,024	4,166
27,800	**27,850**	4,496	4,174	5,038	4,174
27,850	**27,900**	4,510	4,181	5,052	4,181
27,900	**27,950**	4,524	4,189	5,066	4,189
27,950	**28,000**	4,538	4,196	5,080	4,196
28,000					
28,000	**28,050**	4,552	4,204	5,094	4,204
28,050	**28,100**	4,566	4,211	5,108	4,211
28,100	**28,150**	4,580	4,219	5,122	4,219
28,150	**28,200**	4,594	4,226	5,136	4,226
28,200	**28,250**	4,608	4,234	5,150	4,234
28,250	**28,300**	4,622	4,241	5,164	4,241
28,300	**28,350**	4,636	4,249	5,178	4,249
28,350	**28,400**	4,650	4,256	5,192	4,256
28,400	**28,450**	4,664	4,264	5,206	4,264
28,450	**28,500**	4,678	4,271	5,220	4,271
28,500	**28,550**	4,692	4,279	5,234	4,279
28,550	**28,600**	4,706	4,286	5,248	4,286
28,600	**28,650**	4,720	4,294	5,262	4,294
28,650	**28,700**	4,734	4,301	5,276	4,301
28,700	**28,750**	4,748	4,309	5,290	4,309
28,750	**28,800**	4,762	4,316	5,304	4,316
28,800	**28,850**	4,776	4,324	5,318	4,324
28,850	**28,900**	4,790	4,331	5,332	4,331
28,900	**28,950**	4,804	4,339	5,346	4,339
28,950	**29,000**	4,818	4,346	5,360	4,346

If Form 1040A, line 24, is— At least	But less than	And you are— Single	Married filing jointly *	Married filing separately	Head of a household
		Your tax is—			
29,000					
29,000	**29,050**	4,832	4,354	5,374	4,354
29,050	**29,100**	4,846	4,361	5,388	4,361
29,100	**29,150**	4,860	4,369	5,402	4,369
29,150	**29,200**	4,874	4,376	5,416	4,376
29,200	**29,250**	4,888	4,384	5,430	4,384
29,250	**29,300**	4,902	4,391	5,444	4,391
29,300	**29,350**	4,916	4,399	5,458	4,399
29,350	**29,400**	4,930	4,406	5,472	4,406
29,400	**29,450**	4,944	4,414	5,486	4,414
29,450	**29,500**	4,958	4,421	5,500	4,421
29,500	**29,550**	4,972	4,429	5,514	4,429
29,550	**29,600**	4,986	4,436	5,528	4,436
29,600	**29,650**	5,000	4,444	5,542	4,444
29,650	**29,700**	5,014	4,451	5,556	4,451
29,700	**29,750**	5,028	4,459	5,570	4,459
29,750	**29,800**	5,042	4,466	5,584	4,466
29,800	**29,850**	5,056	4,474	5,598	4,474
29,850	**29,900**	5,070	4,481	5,612	4,481
29,900	**29,950**	5,084	4,489	5,626	4,489
29,950	**30,000**	5,098	4,496	5,640	4,496
30,000					
30,000	**30,050**	5,112	4,504	5,654	4,504
30,050	**30,100**	5,126	4,511	5,668	4,511
30,100	**30,150**	5,140	4,519	5,682	4,519
30,150	**30,200**	5,154	4,526	5,696	4,526
30,200	**30,250**	5,168	4,534	5,710	4,534
30,250	**30,300**	5,182	4,541	5,724	4,541
30,300	**30,350**	5,196	4,549	5,738	4,549
30,350	**30,400**	5,210	4,556	5,752	4,556
30,400	**30,450**	5,224	4,564	5,766	4,564
30,450	**30,500**	5,238	4,571	5,780	4,571
30,500	**30,550**	5,252	4,579	5,794	4,579
30,550	**30,600**	5,266	4,586	5,808	4,586
30,600	**30,650**	5,280	4,594	5,822	4,594
30,650	**30,700**	5,294	4,601	5,836	4,601
30,700	**30,750**	5,308	4,609	5,850	4,609
30,750	**30,800**	5,322	4,616	5,864	4,616
30,800	**30,850**	5,336	4,624	5,878	4,624
30,850	**30,900**	5,350	4,631	5,892	4,631
30,900	**30,950**	5,364	4,639	5,906	4,639
30,950	**31,000**	5,378	4,646	5,920	4,646
31,000					
31,000	**31,050**	5,392	4,654	5,934	4,654
31,050	**31,100**	5,406	4,661	5,948	4,661
31,100	**31,150**	5,420	4,669	5,962	4,669
31,150	**31,200**	5,434	4,676	5,976	4,676
31,200	**31,250**	5,448	4,684	5,990	4,684
31,250	**31,300**	5,462	4,691	6,004	4,691
31,300	**31,350**	5,476	4,699	6,018	4,699
31,350	**31,400**	5,490	4,706	6,032	4,706
31,400	**31,450**	5,504	4,714	6,046	4,714
31,450	**31,500**	5,518	4,721	6,060	4,721
31,500	**31,550**	5,532	4,729	6,074	4,729
31,550	**31,600**	5,546	4,736	6,088	4,736
31,600	**31,650**	5,560	4,744	6,102	4,744
31,650	**31,700**	5,574	4,751	6,116	4,751
31,700	**31,750**	5,588	4,759	6,130	4,759
31,750	**31,800**	5,602	4,766	6,144	4,766
31,800	**31,850**	5,616	4,774	6,158	4,774
31,850	**31,900**	5,630	4,781	6,172	4,781
31,900	**31,950**	5,644	4,789	6,186	4,789
31,950	**32,000**	5,658	4,796	6,200	4,796

* This column must also be used by a qualifying widow(er).

Continued on next page

1998 Tax Table—Continued

32,000 / 35,000 / 38,000

At least	But less than	Single	Married filing jointly *	Married filing separately	Head of a household
32,000					
32,000	32,050	5,672	4,804	6,214	4,804
32,050	32,100	5,686	4,811	6,228	4,811
32,100	32,150	5,700	4,819	6,242	4,819
32,150	32,200	5,714	4,826	6,256	4,826
32,200	32,250	5,728	4,834	6,270	4,834
32,250	32,300	5,742	4,841	6,284	4,841
32,300	32,350	5,756	4,849	6,298	4,849
32,350	32,400	5,770	4,856	6,312	4,856
32,400	32,450	5,784	4,864	6,326	4,864
32,450	32,500	5,798	4,871	6,340	4,871
32,500	32,550	5,812	4,879	6,354	4,879
32,550	32,600	5,826	4,886	6,368	4,886
32,600	32,650	5,840	4,894	6,382	4,894
32,650	32,700	5,854	4,901	6,396	4,901
32,700	32,750	5,868	4,909	6,410	4,909
32,750	32,800	5,882	4,916	6,424	4,916
32,800	32,850	5,896	4,924	6,438	4,924
32,850	32,900	5,910	4,931	6,452	4,931
32,900	32,950	5,924	4,939	6,466	4,939
32,950	33,000	5,938	4,946	6,480	4,946
33,000					
33,000	33,050	5,952	4,954	6,494	4,954
33,050	33,100	5,966	4,961	6,508	4,961
33,100	33,150	5,980	4,969	6,522	4,969
33,150	33,200	5,994	4,976	6,536	4,976
33,200	33,250	6,008	4,984	6,550	4,984
33,250	33,300	6,022	4,991	6,564	4,991
33,300	33,350	6,036	4,999	6,578	4,999
33,350	33,400	6,050	5,006	6,592	5,006
33,400	33,450	6,064	5,014	6,606	5,014
33,450	33,500	6,078	5,021	6,620	5,021
33,500	33,550	6,092	5,029	6,634	5,029
33,550	33,600	6,106	5,036	6,648	5,036
33,600	33,650	6,120	5,044	6,662	5,044
33,650	33,700	6,134	5,051	6,676	5,051
33,700	33,750	6,148	5,059	6,690	5,059
33,750	33,800	6,162	5,066	6,704	5,066
33,800	33,850	6,176	5,074	6,718	5,074
33,850	33,900	6,190	5,081	6,732	5,081
33,900	33,950	6,204	5,089	6,746	5,089
33,950	34,000	6,218	5,096	6,760	5,100
34,000					
34,000	34,050	6,232	5,104	6,774	5,114
34,050	34,100	6,246	5,111	6,788	5,128
34,100	34,150	6,260	5,119	6,802	5,142
34,150	34,200	6,274	5,126	6,816	5,156
34,200	34,250	6,288	5,134	6,830	5,170
34,250	34,300	6,302	5,141	6,844	5,184
34,300	34,350	6,316	5,149	6,858	5,198
34,350	34,400	6,330	5,156	6,872	5,212
34,400	34,450	6,344	5,164	6,886	5,226
34,450	34,500	6,358	5,171	6,900	5,240
34,500	34,550	6,372	5,179	6,914	5,254
34,550	34,600	6,386	5,186	6,928	5,268
34,600	34,650	6,400	5,194	6,942	5,282
34,650	34,700	6,414	5,201	6,956	5,296
34,700	34,750	6,428	5,209	6,970	5,310
34,750	34,800	6,442	5,216	6,984	5,324
34,800	34,850	6,456	5,224	6,998	5,338
34,850	34,900	6,470	5,231	7,012	5,352
34,900	34,950	6,484	5,239	7,026	5,366
34,950	35,000	6,498	5,246	7,040	5,380
35,000					
35,000	35,050	6,512	5,254	7,054	5,394
35,050	35,100	6,526	5,261	7,068	5,408
35,100	35,150	6,540	5,269	7,082	5,422
35,150	35,200	6,554	5,276	7,096	5,436
35,200	35,250	6,568	5,284	7,110	5,450
35,250	35,300	6,582	5,291	7,124	5,464
35,300	35,350	6,596	5,299	7,138	5,478
35,350	35,400	6,610	5,306	7,152	5,492
35,400	35,450	6,624	5,314	7,166	5,506
35,450	35,500	6,638	5,321	7,180	5,520
35,500	35,550	6,652	5,329	7,194	5,534
35,550	35,600	6,666	5,336	7,208	5,548
35,600	35,650	6,680	5,344	7,222	5,562
35,650	35,700	6,694	5,351	7,236	5,576
35,700	35,750	6,708	5,359	7,250	5,590
35,750	35,800	6,722	5,366	7,264	5,604
35,800	35,850	6,736	5,374	7,278	5,618
35,850	35,900	6,750	5,381	7,292	5,632
35,900	35,950	6,764	5,389	7,306	5,646
35,950	36,000	6,778	5,396	7,320	5,660
36,000					
36,000	36,050	6,792	5,404	7,334	5,674
36,050	36,100	6,806	5,411	7,348	5,688
36,100	36,150	6,820	5,419	7,362	5,702
36,150	36,200	6,834	5,426	7,376	5,716
36,200	36,250	6,848	5,434	7,390	5,730
36,250	36,300	6,862	5,441	7,404	5,744
36,300	36,350	6,876	5,449	7,418	5,758
36,350	36,400	6,890	5,456	7,432	5,772
36,400	36,450	6,904	5,464	7,446	5,786
36,450	36,500	6,918	5,471	7,460	5,800
36,500	36,550	6,932	5,479	7,474	5,814
36,550	36,600	6,946	5,486	7,488	5,828
36,600	36,650	6,960	5,494	7,502	5,842
36,650	36,700	6,974	5,501	7,516	5,856
36,700	36,750	6,988	5,509	7,530	5,870
36,750	36,800	7,002	5,516	7,544	5,884
36,800	36,850	7,016	5,524	7,558	5,898
36,850	36,900	7,030	5,531	7,572	5,912
36,900	36,950	7,044	5,539	7,586	5,926
36,950	37,000	7,058	5,546	7,600	5,940
37,000					
37,000	37,050	7,072	5,554	7,614	5,954
37,050	37,100	7,086	5,561	7,628	5,968
37,100	37,150	7,100	5,569	7,642	5,982
37,150	37,200	7,114	5,576	7,656	5,996
37,200	37,250	7,128	5,584	7,670	6,010
37,250	37,300	7,142	5,591	7,684	6,024
37,300	37,350	7,156	5,599	7,698	6,038
37,350	37,400	7,170	5,606	7,712	6,052
37,400	37,450	7,184	5,614	7,726	6,066
37,450	37,500	7,198	5,621	7,740	6,080
37,500	37,550	7,212	5,629	7,754	6,094
37,550	37,600	7,226	5,636	7,768	6,108
37,600	37,650	7,240	5,644	7,782	6,122
37,650	37,700	7,254	5,651	7,796	6,136
37,700	37,750	7,268	5,659	7,810	6,150
37,750	37,800	7,282	5,666	7,824	6,164
37,800	37,850	7,296	5,674	7,838	6,178
37,850	37,900	7,310	5,681	7,852	6,192
37,900	37,950	7,324	5,689	7,866	6,206
37,950	38,000	7,338	5,696	7,880	6,220
38,000					
38,000	38,050	7,352	5,704	7,894	6,234
38,050	38,100	7,366	5,711	7,908	6,248
38,100	38,150	7,380	5,719	7,922	6,262
38,150	38,200	7,394	5,726	7,936	6,276
38,200	38,250	7,408	5,734	7,950	6,290
38,250	38,300	7,422	5,741	7,964	6,304
38,300	38,350	7,436	5,749	7,978	6,318
38,350	38,400	7,450	5,756	7,992	6,332
38,400	38,450	7,464	5,764	8,006	6,346
38,450	38,500	7,478	5,771	8,020	6,360
38,500	38,550	7,492	5,779	8,034	6,374
38,550	38,600	7,506	5,786	8,048	6,388
38,600	38,650	7,520	5,794	8,062	6,402
38,650	38,700	7,534	5,801	8,076	6,416
38,700	38,750	7,548	5,809	8,090	6,430
38,750	38,800	7,562	5,816	8,104	6,444
38,800	38,850	7,576	5,824	8,118	6,458
38,850	38,900	7,590	5,831	8,132	6,472
38,900	38,950	7,604	5,839	8,146	6,486
38,950	39,000	7,618	5,846	8,160	6,500
39,000					
39,000	39,050	7,632	5,854	8,174	6,514
39,050	39,100	7,646	5,861	8,188	6,528
39,100	39,150	7,660	5,869	8,202	6,542
39,150	39,200	7,674	5,876	8,216	6,556
39,200	39,250	7,688	5,884	8,230	6,570
39,250	39,300	7,702	5,891	8,244	6,584
39,300	39,350	7,716	5,899	8,258	6,598
39,350	39,400	7,730	5,906	8,272	6,612
39,400	39,450	7,744	5,914	8,286	6,626
39,450	39,500	7,758	5,921	8,300	6,640
39,500	39,550	7,772	5,929	8,314	6,654
39,550	39,600	7,786	5,936	8,328	6,668
39,600	39,650	7,800	5,944	8,342	6,682
39,650	39,700	7,814	5,951	8,356	6,696
39,700	39,750	7,828	5,959	8,370	6,710
39,750	39,800	7,842	5,966	8,384	6,724
39,800	39,850	7,856	5,974	8,398	6,738
39,850	39,900	7,870	5,981	8,412	6,752
39,900	39,950	7,884	5,989	8,426	6,766
39,950	40,000	7,898	5,996	8,440	6,780
40,000					
40,000	40,050	7,912	6,004	8,454	6,794
40,050	40,100	7,926	6,011	8,468	6,808
40,100	40,150	7,940	6,019	8,482	6,822
40,150	40,200	7,954	6,026	8,496	6,836
40,200	40,250	7,968	6,034	8,510	6,850
40,250	40,300	7,982	6,041	8,524	6,864
40,300	40,350	7,996	6,049	8,538	6,878
40,350	40,400	8,010	6,056	8,552	6,892
40,400	40,450	8,024	6,064	8,566	6,906
40,450	40,500	8,038	6,071	8,580	6,920
40,500	40,550	8,052	6,079	8,594	6,934
40,550	40,600	8,066	6,086	8,608	6,948
40,600	40,650	8,080	6,094	8,622	6,962
40,650	40,700	8,094	6,101	8,636	6,976
40,700	40,750	8,108	6,109	8,650	6,990
40,750	40,800	8,122	6,116	8,664	7,004
40,800	40,850	8,136	6,124	8,678	7,018
40,850	40,900	8,150	6,131	8,692	7,032
40,900	40,950	8,164	6,139	8,706	7,046
40,950	41,000	8,178	6,146	8,720	7,060

* This column must also be used by a qualifying widow(er).

Continued on next page

1998 Tax Table—Continued

41,000 – 44,000

At least	But less than	Single	Married filing jointly*	Married filing separately	Head of a household
41,000					
41,000	41,050	8,192	6,154	8,734	7,074
41,050	41,100	8,206	6,161	8,748	7,088
41,100	41,150	8,220	6,169	8,762	7,102
41,150	41,200	8,234	6,176	8,776	7,116
41,200	41,250	8,248	6,184	8,790	7,130
41,250	41,300	8,262	6,191	8,804	7,144
41,300	41,350	8,276	6,199	8,818	7,158
41,350	41,400	8,290	6,206	8,832	7,172
41,400	41,450	8,304	6,214	8,846	7,186
41,450	41,500	8,318	6,221	8,860	7,200
41,500	41,550	8,332	6,229	8,874	7,214
41,550	41,600	8,346	6,236	8,888	7,228
41,600	41,650	8,360	6,244	8,902	7,242
41,650	41,700	8,374	6,251	8,916	7,256
41,700	41,750	8,388	6,259	8,930	7,270
41,750	41,800	8,402	6,266	8,944	7,284
41,800	41,850	8,416	6,274	8,958	7,298
41,850	41,900	8,430	6,281	8,972	7,312
41,900	41,950	8,444	6,289	8,986	7,326
41,950	42,000	8,458	6,296	9,000	7,340
42,000					
42,000	42,050	8,472	6,304	9,014	7,354
42,050	42,100	8,486	6,311	9,028	7,368
42,100	42,150	8,500	6,319	9,042	7,382
42,150	42,200	8,514	6,326	9,056	7,396
42,200	42,250	8,528	6,334	9,070	7,410
42,250	42,300	8,542	6,341	9,084	7,424
42,300	42,350	8,556	6,349	9,098	7,438
42,350	42,400	8,570	6,360	9,112	7,452
42,400	42,450	8,584	6,374	9,126	7,466
42,450	42,500	8,598	6,388	9,140	7,480
42,500	42,550	8,612	6,402	9,154	7,494
42,550	42,600	8,626	6,416	9,168	7,508
42,600	42,650	8,640	6,430	9,182	7,522
42,650	42,700	8,654	6,444	9,196	7,536
42,700	42,750	8,668	6,458	9,210	7,550
42,750	42,800	8,682	6,472	9,224	7,564
42,800	42,850	8,696	6,486	9,238	7,578
42,850	42,900	8,710	6,500	9,252	7,592
42,900	42,950	8,724	6,514	9,266	7,606
42,950	43,000	8,738	6,528	9,280	7,620
43,000					
43,000	43,050	8,752	6,542	9,294	7,634
43,050	43,100	8,766	6,556	9,308	7,648
43,100	43,150	8,780	6,570	9,322	7,662
43,150	43,200	8,794	6,584	9,336	7,676
43,200	43,250	8,808	6,598	9,350	7,690
43,250	43,300	8,822	6,612	9,364	7,704
43,300	43,350	8,836	6,626	9,378	7,718
43,350	43,400	8,850	6,640	9,392	7,732
43,400	43,450	8,864	6,654	9,406	7,746
43,450	43,500	8,878	6,668	9,420	7,760
43,500	43,550	8,892	6,682	9,434	7,774
43,550	43,600	8,906	6,696	9,448	7,788
43,600	43,650	8,920	6,710	9,462	7,802
43,650	43,700	8,934	6,724	9,476	7,816
43,700	43,750	8,948	6,738	9,490	7,830
43,750	43,800	8,962	6,752	9,504	7,844
43,800	43,850	8,976	6,766	9,518	7,858
43,850	43,900	8,990	6,780	9,532	7,872
43,900	43,950	9,004	6,794	9,546	7,886
43,950	44,000	9,018	6,808	9,560	7,900

44,000 – 47,000

At least	But less than	Single	Married filing jointly*	Married filing separately	Head of a household
44,000					
44,000	44,050	9,032	6,822	9,574	7,914
44,050	44,100	9,046	6,836	9,588	7,928
44,100	44,150	9,060	6,850	9,602	7,942
44,150	44,200	9,074	6,864	9,616	7,956
44,200	44,250	9,088	6,878	9,630	7,970
44,250	44,300	9,102	6,892	9,644	7,984
44,300	44,350	9,116	6,906	9,658	7,998
44,350	44,400	9,130	6,920	9,672	8,012
44,400	44,450	9,144	6,934	9,686	8,026
44,450	44,500	9,158	6,948	9,700	8,040
44,500	44,550	9,172	6,962	9,714	8,054
44,550	44,600	9,186	6,976	9,728	8,068
44,600	44,650	9,200	6,990	9,742	8,082
44,650	44,700	9,214	7,004	9,756	8,096
44,700	44,750	9,228	7,018	9,770	8,110
44,750	44,800	9,242	7,032	9,784	8,124
44,800	44,850	9,256	7,046	9,798	8,138
44,850	44,900	9,270	7,060	9,812	8,152
44,900	44,950	9,284	7,074	9,826	8,166
44,950	45,000	9,298	7,088	9,840	8,180
45,000					
45,000	45,050	9,312	7,102	9,854	8,194
45,050	45,100	9,326	7,116	9,868	8,208
45,100	45,150	9,340	7,130	9,882	8,222
45,150	45,200	9,354	7,144	9,896	8,236
45,200	45,250	9,368	7,158	9,910	8,250
45,250	45,300	9,382	7,172	9,924	8,264
45,300	45,350	9,396	7,186	9,938	8,278
45,350	45,400	9,410	7,200	9,952	8,292
45,400	45,450	9,424	7,214	9,966	8,306
45,450	45,500	9,438	7,228	9,980	8,320
45,500	45,550	9,452	7,242	9,994	8,334
45,550	45,600	9,466	7,256	10,008	8,348
45,600	45,650	9,480	7,270	10,022	8,362
45,650	45,700	9,494	7,284	10,036	8,376
45,700	45,750	9,508	7,298	10,050	8,390
45,750	45,800	9,522	7,312	10,064	8,404
45,800	45,850	9,536	7,326	10,078	8,418
45,850	45,900	9,550	7,340	10,092	8,432
45,900	45,950	9,564	7,354	10,106	8,446
45,950	46,000	9,578	7,368	10,120	8,460
46,000					
46,000	46,050	9,592	7,382	10,134	8,474
46,050	46,100	9,606	7,396	10,148	8,488
46,100	46,150	9,620	7,410	10,162	8,502
46,150	46,200	9,634	7,424	10,176	8,516
46,200	46,250	9,648	7,438	10,190	8,530
46,250	46,300	9,662	7,452	10,204	8,544
46,300	46,350	9,676	7,466	10,218	8,558
46,350	46,400	9,690	7,480	10,232	8,572
46,400	46,450	9,704	7,494	10,246	8,586
46,450	46,500	9,718	7,508	10,260	8,600
46,500	46,550	9,732	7,522	10,274	8,614
46,550	46,600	9,746	7,536	10,288	8,628
46,600	46,650	9,760	7,550	10,302	8,642
46,650	46,700	9,774	7,564	10,316	8,656
46,700	46,750	9,788	7,578	10,330	8,670
46,750	46,800	9,802	7,592	10,344	8,684
46,800	46,850	9,816	7,606	10,358	8,698
46,850	46,900	9,830	7,620	10,372	8,712
46,900	46,950	9,844	7,634	10,386	8,726
46,950	47,000	9,858	7,648	10,400	8,740

47,000 – 50,000

At least	But less than	Single	Married filing jointly*	Married filing separately	Head of a household
47,000					
47,000	47,050	9,872	7,662	10,414	8,754
47,050	47,100	9,886	7,676	10,428	8,768
47,100	47,150	9,900	7,690	10,442	8,782
47,150	47,200	9,914	7,704	10,456	8,796
47,200	47,250	9,928	7,718	10,470	8,810
47,250	47,300	9,942	7,732	10,484	8,824
47,300	47,350	9,956	7,746	10,498	8,838
47,350	47,400	9,970	7,760	10,512	8,852
47,400	47,450	9,984	7,774	10,526	8,866
47,450	47,500	9,998	7,788	10,540	8,880
47,500	47,550	10,012	7,802	10,554	8,894
47,550	47,600	10,026	7,816	10,568	8,908
47,600	47,650	10,040	7,830	10,582	8,922
47,650	47,700	10,054	7,844	10,596	8,936
47,700	47,750	10,068	7,858	10,610	8,950
47,750	47,800	10,082	7,872	10,624	8,964
47,800	47,850	10,096	7,886	10,638	8,978
47,850	47,900	10,110	7,900	10,652	8,992
47,900	47,950	10,124	7,914	10,666	9,006
47,950	48,000	10,138	7,928	10,680	9,020
48,000					
48,000	48,050	10,152	7,942	10,694	9,034
48,050	48,100	10,166	7,956	10,708	9,048
48,100	48,150	10,180	7,970	10,722	9,062
48,150	48,200	10,194	7,984	10,736	9,076
48,200	48,250	10,208	7,998	10,750	9,090
48,250	48,300	10,222	8,012	10,764	9,104
48,300	48,350	10,236	8,026	10,778	9,118
48,350	48,400	10,250	8,040	10,792	9,132
48,400	48,450	10,264	8,054	10,806	9,146
48,450	48,500	10,278	8,068	10,820	9,160
48,500	48,550	10,292	8,082	10,834	9,174
48,550	48,600	10,306	8,096	10,848	9,188
48,600	48,650	10,320	8,110	10,862	9,202
48,650	48,700	10,334	8,124	10,876	9,216
48,700	48,750	10,348	8,138	10,890	9,230
48,750	48,800	10,362	8,152	10,904	9,244
48,800	48,850	10,376	8,166	10,918	9,258
48,850	48,900	10,390	8,180	10,932	9,272
48,900	48,950	10,404	8,194	10,946	9,286
48,950	49,000	10,418	8,208	10,960	9,300
49,000					
49,000	49,050	10,432	8,222	10,974	9,314
49,050	49,100	10,446	8,236	10,988	9,328
49,100	49,150	10,460	8,250	11,002	9,342
49,150	49,200	10,474	8,264	11,016	9,356
49,200	49,250	10,488	8,278	11,030	9,370
49,250	49,300	10,502	8,292	11,044	9,384
49,300	49,350	10,516	8,306	11,058	9,398
49,350	49,400	10,530	8,320	11,072	9,412
49,400	49,450	10,544	8,334	11,086	9,426
49,450	49,500	10,558	8,348	11,100	9,440
49,500	49,550	10,572	8,362	11,114	9,454
49,550	49,600	10,586	8,376	11,128	9,468
49,600	49,650	10,600	8,390	11,142	9,482
49,650	49,700	10,614	8,404	11,156	9,496
49,700	49,750	10,628	8,418	11,170	9,510
49,750	49,800	10,642	8,432	11,184	9,524
49,800	49,850	10,656	8,446	11,198	9,538
49,850	49,900	10,670	8,460	11,212	9,552
49,900	49,950	10,684	8,474	11,226	9,566
49,950	50,000	10,698	8,488	11,240	9,580

* This column must also be used by a qualifying widow(er).

(50,000 or over— use Form 1040)

Appendix

OVERVIEW

The Appendix provides information about situations that require additional forms. Discuss these forms if they are appropriate for your students.

- **Schedule 1**

    For taxpayers with more than $400 in taxable income or dividends. (An explanation and blank form are provided.)

- **Schedule 2**

    For qualifying taxpayers with child and dependent care expenses. (An explanation, blank form, and sample exercise are provided.)

- **Schedule EIC (earned income credit)**

    For taxpayers who qualify for the earned income credit. (An explanation, blank form, and sample exercise are provided.)

SCHEDULE 1

Schedule 1 is for taxpayers of any age who:

- had over $400 in taxable interest income

OR

- had Series EE U.S. savings bonds and are claiming the exclusion of interest for these savings

OR

- had over $400 in dividends.

On the top line of this form, print your first and last name. Also write your Social Security number.

Part I   1. List the names of all of the banks that paid you interest. Fill in the amount of interest you received from each bank.

        2. Add all of the amounts listed in 1.

        3. Total the amount of excludable interest you received on your Series EE savings bonds.

        4. Subtract 3 from 2. Write this amount on this form, and on Form 1040A, line 8a.

Part II   5. List the names of all of the companies that paid you dividends on their stocks or bonds. Also fill in the amount of dividends you received from each company.

        6. Add all of the amounts listed in 5. Write this amount on this form, and on Form 1040A, line 9.

SCHEDULE 1—SIDE 1

Schedule 1 **(Form 1040A)**	Department of the Treasury—Internal Revenue Service **Interest and Ordinary Dividends** **for Form 1040A Filers**	**1998**	OMB No. 1545-0085

Name(s) shown on Form 1040A	**Your social security number**

Part I

Interest

(See pages 24 and 56.)

Note: *If you received a Form 1099–INT, Form 1099–OID, or substitute statement from a brokerage firm, enter the firm's name and the total interest shown on that form.*

1 List name of payer. If any interest is from a seller-financed mortgage and the buyer used the property as a personal residence, see page 56 and list this interest first. Also, show that buyer's social security number and address.

	Amount
1	

2 Add the amounts on line 1. .... **2**

3 Excludable interest on series EE U.S. savings bonds issued after 1989 from Form 8815, line 14. You **must** attach Form 8815 to Form 1040A. **3**

4 Subtract line 3 from line 2. Enter the result here and on Form 1040A, line 8a. **4**

Part II

Ordinary dividends

(See pages 24 and 56.)

Note: *If you received a Form 1099–DIV or substitute statement from a brokerage firm, enter the firm's name and the ordinary dividends shown on that form.*

5 List name of payer

	Amount
5	

6 Add the amounts on line 5. Enter the total here and on Form 1040A, line 9. **6**

For Paperwork Reduction Act Notice, see Form 1040A instructions.   Cat. No. 12075R   **1998 Schedule 1 (Form 1040A)**

SCHEDULE 2

Schedule 2 is for taxpayers who:

- paid for the care of one or more qualifying persons

AND

- lived with the qualifying person or persons

AND

- earned income during the year

AND

- paid for the care in order to be able to work or look for a job

AND

- are not using the filing status of married couple, filing separately.

A "qualifying person" is:

- your dependent who was under the age of 13 when the care was provided and for whom you claim an exemption on Form 1040A

OR

- your spouse who was physically or mentally unable to care for himself/herself

OR

- your dependent who was unable to care for himself/herself and for whom you claim an exemption on Form 1040A.

If you paid child or dependent care expenses for at least one qualifying person, you should complete Schedule 2.

On the top line of this form, print your first and last name. Also write your Social Security number.

In Part 1, you will need to provide information about the people or organizations that provided the child or dependent care.

Part I   1a.   Print the name of each provider.

1b.   Print the address of each provider.

1c.   Write the Social Security number or Employer Identification Number of each provider.

1d.   Write the total amount paid to each provider.

If you received employer-provided dependent care benefits, complete Part III.

If you did not receive employer-provided dependent care benefits, complete only Part II.

Part II   2a.   Print the first and last name of each qualifying person.

2b.   Print the Social Security number of each qualifying person.

2c.   Print the amount of expenses you paid for each qualifying person.

3.   Add the amounts listed in 2c. Do not write more than $2,400 for one qualifying person or $4,800 for two or more persons.

4.   Write the amount of your earned income (from your W-2 form).

5.   If you are married and filing a joint return, write the amount of your spouse's earned income. Otherwise, write your earned income from line 4.

6.   Compare the amounts on lines 3, 4, and 5. Write the smallest of the three amounts on line 6.

7.   Write the amount from Form 1040A, line 19 on line 7 of Schedule 2.

8.   Find the decimal amount that applies to the amount on line 7.

9.   Multiply the amount on line 6 by the decimal amount on line 8. Write the result on line 9.

10.   Write the amount on line 9 on Form 1040A, line 26.

1040A AND SCHEDULE 2

ACTIVITY: Practice filling out the form for Margaret Murphy's family.

Margaret Murphy is a computer programmer. She is single and she earned $26,500. She did not earn any interest during the year, and her itemized deductions were less than $500. She had $2,860 of federal income tax withheld from her pay. Her daughter, Colleen, is eight years old. Margaret paid the YMCA to care for her daughter. Her child-care expenses for the year totaled $3,000.

She lives at 418 Main Street, Westwyck, Massachusetts 05000. She wants to contribute to the Presidential Campaign Election fund.

The EIN of the YMCA is 94-1654052. Its address is 615 49th Street, Westwyck, Massachusetts 05000.

Margaret's Social Security number is 600-55-4213. Colleen's Social Security number is 600-33-3124.

W-2—MARGARET MURPHY

a Control number		OMB No. 1545-0008

b Employer identification number 9516464464	**1** Wages, tips, other compensation 26,500.00	**2** Federal income tax withheld 2,860.00
c Employer's name, address, and ZIP code Superior Computer Services 14 Gates Avenue Suite 301 Westwyck, MA 05000	**3** Social security wages 26,500.00	**4** Social security tax withheld 1,643.00
	5 Medicare wages and tips 26,500.00	**6** Medicare tax withheld 384.25
	7 Social security tips	**8** Allocated tips
d Employee's social security number 600-55-4213	**9** Advance EIC payment	**10** Dependent care benefits
e Employee's name (first, middle initial, last) Margaret Murphy 418 Main Street Westwyck, MA 05000	**11** Nonqualified plans	**12** Benefits included in box 1
	13 See instrs. for box 13	**14** Other

15 Statutory employee ☐	Deceased ☐	Pension plan ☐	Legal rep. ☐	Deferred compensation ☐

f Employee's address and ZIP code

16 State	Employer's state I.D. no.	**17** State wages, tips, etc.	**18** State income tax	**19** Locality name	**20** Local wages, tips, etc.	**21** Local income tax
MA		26,500.00	250.00			

1040A—PAGE 1

| Form **1040A** | Department of the Treasury–Internal Revenue Service **U.S. Individual Income Tax Return** | **1998** | IRS Use Only–Do not write or staple in this space. |

OMB No. 1545-0085

Label
(See page 18.)

Use the IRS label.
Otherwise, please print or type.

L A B E L   H E R E

Your first name and initial **Margaret**   Last name **Murphy**

Your social security number **600 55 4213**

If a joint return, spouse's first name and initial   Last name

Spouse's social security number

Home address (number and street). If you have a P.O. box, see page 19. **418 Main Street**   Apt. no.

City, town or post office, state, and ZIP code. If you have a foreign address, see page 19. **Westwyck, MA 05000**

▲ **IMPORTANT!** ▲
You **must** enter your SSN(s) above.

Presidential Election Campaign Fund (See page 19.)
Do you want $3 to go to this fund? . . . . [Yes ☒] [No]
If a joint return, does your spouse want $3 to go to this fund?

Note: Checking "Yes" will not change your tax or reduce your refund.

Filing status

Check only one box.

1 ☐ Single
2 ☐ Married filing joint return (even if only one had income)
3 ☐ Married filing separate return. Enter spouse's social security number above and full name here. ▶
4 ☒ Head of household (with qualifying person). (See page 20.) If the qualifying person is a child but not your dependent, enter this child's name here. ▶
5 ☐ Qualifying widow(er) with dependent child (year spouse died ▶ 19). (See page 21.)

Exemptions

If more than seven dependents, see page 21.

6a ☐ **Yourself.** If your parent (or someone else) can claim you as a dependent on his or her tax return, **do not** check box 6a.

b ☐ **Spouse**

c **Dependents:**

(1) First name Last name	(2) Dependent's social security number	(3) Dependent's relationship to you	(4) ✓ if qualified child for child tax credit (see page 22)
Colleen Murphy	600 33 3124	daughter	☑
			☐
			☐
			☐
			☐
			☐
			☐

No. of boxes checked on 6a and 6b **1**

No. of your children on 6c who:
● lived with you **1**
● did not live with you due to divorce or separation (see page 23) **0**

Dependents on 6c not entered above **0**

d Total number of exemptions claimed.

Add numbers entered on lines above **2**

Income

Attach Copy B of your Forms W-2 and 1099-R here.

If you did not get a W-2, see page 24.

Enclose, but do not staple, any payment.

7	Wages, salaries, tips, etc. Attach Form(s) W-2.		7	26,500 00
8a	**Taxable** interest. Attach Schedule 1 if required.		8a	0 00
b	**Tax-exempt** interest. DO NOT include on line 8a.	8b		
9	Ordinary dividends. Attach Schedule 1 if required.		9	0 00
10a	Total IRA distributions. 10a	**10b** Taxable amount (see page 24).	10b	0 00
11a	Total pensions and annuities. 11a	**11b** Taxable amount (see page 25).	11b	0 00
12	Unemployment compensation.		12	0 00
13a	Social security benefits. 13a	**13b** Taxable amount (see page 27).	13b	0 00
14	Add lines 7 through 13b (far right column). This is your **total income.** ▶		14	26,500 00

Adjusted gross income

15	IRA deduction (see page 28).	15	0 00	
16	Student loan interest deduction (see page 28).	16	0 00	
17	Add lines 15 and 16. These are your **total adjustments.**	17		0 00
18	Subtract line 17 from line 14. This is your **adjusted gross income.** If under $30,095 (under $10,030 if a child did not live with you), see the EIC instructions on page 36. ▶	18		26,500 00

For Disclosure, Privacy Act, and Paperwork Reduction Act Notice, see page 49.   Cat. No. 11327A   **1998 Form 1040A**

1040A—PAGE 2

1998 Form 1040A page 2

Taxable income	**19**	Enter the amount from line 18.	19	26,500 00

20a Check if: ☐ **You** were 65 or older ☐ Blind ☐ **Spouse** was 65 or older ☐ Blind Enter number of boxes checked ▶ 20a ☐

b If you are married filing separately and your spouse itemizes deductions, see page 30 and check here . . . . . ▶ 20b ☐

21 Enter the **standard deduction** for your filing status. **But** see page 31 if you checked any box on line 20a or 20b **OR** if someone can claim you as a dependent.
● Single—$4,250 ● Married filing jointly or Qualifying widow(er)—$7,100
● Head of household—$6,250 ● Married filing separately—$3,550 | 21 | 6,250 00 |

22	Subtract line 21 from line 19. If line 21 is more than line 19, enter -0-.	22	20,250 00
23	Multiply $2,700 by the total number of exemptions claimed on line 6d.	23	5,400 00
24	Subtract line 23 from line 22. If line 23 is more than line 22, enter -0-. This is your **taxable income.** ▶	24	14,850 00

Tax, credits, and payments

25	Find the tax on the amount on line 24 (see page 31).		25	2,231 00
26	Credit for child and dependent care expenses. Attach Schedule 2.	26	504 00	
27	Credit for the elderly or the disabled. Attach Schedule 3.	27		
28	Child tax credit (see page 32).	28	400 00	
29	Education credits. Attach Form 8863.	29		
30	Adoption credit. Attach Form 8839.	30		
31	Add lines 26 through 30. These are your **total credits.**	31		904 00
32	Subtract line 31 from line 25. If line 31 is more than line 25, enter -0-.	32		1,327 00
33	Advance earned income credit payments from Form(s) W-2.	33		0 00
34	Add lines 32 and 33. This is your **total tax.** ▶	34		1,327 00
35	Total Federal income tax withheld from Forms W-2 and 1099.	35	2,860 00	
36	1998 estimated tax payments and amount applied from 1997 return.	36	0 00	
37a	**Earned income credit.** Attach Schedule EIC if you have a qualifying child.	37a	0 00	
b	Nontaxable earned income: amount ▶ and type ▶			
38	Additional child tax credit. Attach Form 8812.	38	0 00	
39	Add lines 35, 36, 37a, and 38. These are your **total payments.** ▶	39		2,860 00

Refund
Have it directly deposited! See page 43 and fill in 41b, 41c, and 41d.

40	If line 39 is more than line 34, subtract line 34 from line 39. This is the amount you **overpaid.**	40	1,533 00
41a	Amount of line 40 you want **refunded to you.**	41a	1,533 00

b Routing number ☐☐☐☐☐☐☐☐☐ **c** Type: ☐ Checking ☐ Savings
d Account number ☐☐☐☐☐☐☐☐☐☐☐☐☐☐☐☐☐

42 Amount of line 40 you want **applied to your 1999 estimated tax.** 42

Amount you owe

43 If line 34 is more than line 39, subtract line 39 from line 34. This is the **amount you owe.** For details on how to pay, see page 44. 43

44 Estimated tax penalty (see page 44). 44

Sign here
Joint return? See page 19. Keep a copy for your records.

Under penalties of perjury, I declare that I have examined this return and accompanying schedules and statements, and to the best of my knowledge and belief, they are true, correct, and accurately list all amounts and sources of income I received during the tax year. Declaration of preparer (other than the taxpayer) is based on all information of which the preparer has any knowledge.

Your signature | Date | Your occupation | Daytime telephone number (optional)
Spouse's signature. If joint return, BOTH must sign. | Date | Spouse's occupation | ( )

Paid preparer's use only
Preparer's signature ▶ | Date | Check if self-employed ☐ | Preparer's social security no.
Firm's name (or yours if self-employed) and address ▶ | | EIN | ZIP code

SCHEDULE 2—PAGE 1

Schedule 2 **(Form 1040A)**	Department of the Treasury—Internal Revenue Service **Child and Dependent Care** **Expenses for Form 1040A Filers** (99) **1998**

OMB No. 1545-0085

Name(s) shown on Form 1040A
Margaret Murphy

Your social security number
600 55 4213

Before you begin, you need to understand the following terms. See **Definitions** on page 57.
● Dependent Care Benefits ● Qualifying Person(s) ● Qualified Expenses ● Earned Income

Part I

Persons or organizations who provided the care

You MUST complete this part.

1	(a) Care provider's name	(b) Address (number, street, apt. no., city, state, and ZIP code)	(c) Identifying number (SSN or EIN)	(d) Amount paid (see page 58)
	YMCA	615 49th St. Westwyck, MA 05000	941 65 4052	3,000 00

(If you need more space, use the bottom of page 2.)

Did you receive **dependent care benefits?**	**No** ⟶ Complete only Part II below.
	Yes ⟶ Complete Part III on the back next.

Caution: *If the care was provided in your home, you may owe employment taxes. If you do, you must use Form 1040. See* **Schedule H** *and its instructions for details.*

Part II

Credit for child and dependent care expenses

2 Information about your **qualifying person(s).** If you have more than two qualifying persons, see page 58.

(a) Qualifying person's name		(b) Qualifying person's social security number	(c) **Qualified expenses** you incurred and paid in 1998 for the person listed in column (a)
First	Last		
Colleen	Murphy	600 33 3124	3,000 00

3 Add the amounts in column (c) of line 2. DO NOT enter more than $2,400 for one qualifying person or $4,800 for two or more persons. If you completed Part III, enter the amount from line 24. ... **3** | 2,400 00

4 Enter YOUR **earned income.** ... **4** | 26,500 00

5 If married filing a joint return, enter YOUR SPOUSE'S earned income (if your spouse was a student or was disabled, see page 59); **all others,** enter the amount from line 4. ... **5** | 26,500 00

6 Enter the **smallest** of line 3, 4, or 5. ... **6** | 2,400 00

7 Enter the amount from Form 1040A, line 19.   **7** 26,500 00

8 Enter on line 8 the decimal amount shown below that applies to the amount on line 7.

If line 7 is—		Decimal amount is	If line 7 is—		Decimal amount is
Over	But not over		Over	But not over	
$0	10,000	.30	$20,000	22,000	.24
10,000	12,000	.29	22,000	24,000	.23
12,000	14,000	.28	24,000	26,000	.22
14,000	16,000	.27	26,000	28,000	.21
16,000	18,000	.26	28,000	No limit	.20
18,000	20,000	.25			

8 | .21

9 Multiply **line 6** by the decimal amount on line 8. Enter the result. Then, see page 59 for the amount of credit to enter on Form 1040A, line 26. ... **9** | 504 00

For Paperwork Reduction Act Notice, see Form 1040A instructions. | Cat. No. 107491 | **1998 Schedule 2 (Form 1040A)**

SCHEDULE 2—PAGE 2

1998 Schedule 2 (Form 1040A) page 2

Part III

Dependent care benefits

10 Enter the total amount of **dependent care benefits** you received for 1998. This amount should be shown in box 10 of your W-2 form(s). DO NOT include amounts that were reported to you as wages in box 1 of Form(s) W-2.   10

11 Enter the amount forfeited, if any. See page 59.   11

12 Subtract line 11 from line 10.   12

13 Enter the total amount of **qualified expenses** incurred in 1998 for the care of the qualifying person(s).   13

14 Enter the **smaller** of line 12 or 13.   14

15 Enter YOUR **earned income.**   15

16 If married filing a joint return, enter YOUR SPOUSE'S earned income (if your spouse was a student or was disabled, see the instructions for line 5); if married filing a separate return, see the instructions for the amount to enter; **all others,** enter the amount from line 15.   16

17 Enter the **smallest** of line 14, 15, or 16.   17

18 **Excluded benefits.** Enter here the **smaller** of the following:
● The amount from line 17, or
● $5,000 ($2,500 if married filing a separate return **and** you were required to enter your spouse's earned income on line 16).   18

19 **Taxable benefits.** Subtract line 18 from line 12. Also, include this amount on Form 1040A, line 7. In the space to the left of line 7, enter "DCB."   19

To claim the child and dependent care credit, complete lines 20–24 below.

20 Enter $2,400 ($4,800 if two or more qualifying persons).   20

21 Enter the amount from line 18.   21

22 Subtract line 21 from line 20. If zero or less, **STOP.** You cannot take the credit. **Exception.** If you paid 1997 expenses in 1998, see the instructions for line 9.   22

23 Complete line 2 on the front of this schedule. DO NOT include in column (c) any excluded benefits shown on line 18 above. Then, add the amounts in column (c) and enter the total here.   23

24 Enter the **smaller** of line 22 or 23 here. Also, enter this amount on line 3 on the front of this schedule and complete lines 4–9.   24

1040A—CHILD TAX CREDIT WORKSHEET

Child Tax Credit Worksheet–Line 28

▶ Keep for your records.

Do Not File

1. $400.00 _____1_____ . Multiply and enter the result . . . . 1. __400|00__

   ▲

   Enter number of qualifying children (see page 32)

2. Enter the amount from Form 1040A, line 19 . . . . . 2. __26,500|00__

3. Is line 2 above more than $55,000?

   ☒ **No.** Skip lines 3 through 5, enter -0- on line 6, and go to line 7.

   ☐ **Yes.** Enter: $75,000 if single, head of household, or qualifying widow(er); $110,000 if married filing jointly; $55,000 if married filing separately . . . . . 3. _____

4. Subtract line 3 from line 2. If zero or less, enter -0- here and on line 6, and go to line 7 . . . . 4. _____

5. Divide line 4 by $1,000. If the result is not a whole number, round it up to the next higher whole number (for example, round 0.01 to 1) . . . . 5. _____

6. Multiply $50 by the number on line 5 . . . . 6. __0|00__

7. Subtract line 6 from line 1. If zero or less, **stop here; you cannot** take this credit . 7. __400|00__

8. Enter the amount from Form 1040A, line 25 . . . . . 8. __2,231|00__

9. Is line 1 above more than $800?

   ☐ **No.** Add the amounts from Form 1040A, lines 26, 27, and 29. Enter the total.

   ☐ **Yes.** Enter the amount from the worksheet on page 34. } 9. __504|00__

10. Subtract line 9 above from line 8 . . . . 10. __1,727|00__

11. **Child tax credit.** Enter the **smaller** of line 7 or line 10 here and on Form 1040A, line 28 ▶ 11. __400|00__

TIP *If line 1 above is more than $800, you may be able to take the **Additional Child Tax Credit**. See page 32.*

SCHEDULE EIC

Schedule EIC (earned income credit) is for a taxpayer of any age who:

- worked and earned less than $30,095

AND

- completed Form 1040A, indicating that line 8 was less than $30,095

AND

- is not using the filing status of married couple, filing separately

AND

- has at least one qualifying child

AND

- is not a qualifying child himself/herself.

A "qualifying child" is your:

- ☐ son
- ☐ daughter
- ☐ adopted child
- ☐ grandchild
- ☐ stepchild
- ☐ foster child
- who was under the age of 19

OR

- under the age of 24 and a full-time student

OR

- any age and permanently and totally disabled

AND

- who lived with you in the United States for more than six months (or all year if a foster child).

If you have at least one qualifying child, and fulfill all of the requirements listed before, you may complete Schedule EIC.

On the top line of this form, print your first and last name. Also write your Social Security number.

You will need to provide information about a maximum of two qualifying children.

1. Print each child's first name and last name.

2. Write each child's year of birth.

3a. For a child born before 1980, check if the child was a student under the age of 24.

3b. For a child born before 1980, check if the child was disabled.

4. Write the child's Social Security number.

5. Indicate the child's relationship to you.

6. Indicate the number of months the child lived with you in the United States.

If you want the IRS to calculate your credit for you, write "EIC" next to line 37a of Form 1040A.

If you want to calculate your credit yourself, you will need to fill out the worksheet provided with the 1040A instructions.

1040A AND EIC PRACTICE

ACTIVITY: Have students fill out the form for Bill Smith and his family.

Jamal Answar earned $18,000 as a factory worker. His wife, Radira, stayed home to care for the children. Their son, Jumur, is two years old. Their daughter, Lale, is one year old.

They have no savings account and $1,000 in deductions. Jamal had $400 withheld from his pay.

They are eligible to receive the earned income credit (EIC). They do not have health insurance.

Jamal and Radira live at 257 8th Street, Apt. 110, Atlanta, Georgia 30000. They want to contribute to the Presidential Election Campaign fund. The Social Security numbers for the family are:

Jamal:	008-54-1482
Radira:	008-07-8304
Jumur:	008-71-3418
Lale:	008-33-2596

W-2—JAMAL ANSWAR

a Control number		Void ☐	**For Official Use Only** ►	

b Employer identification number 9514545454	**1** Wages, tips, other compensation 18,000.00	**2** Federal income tax withheld 400.00
c Employer's name, address, and ZIP code Consolidated Electronics, Inc. 965 Edison Drive Atlanta, GA 30000	**3** Social security wages 18,000.00	**4** Social security tax withheld 1,116.00
	5 Medicare wages and tips 18,000.00	**6** Medicare tax withheld 261.00
	7 Social security tips	**8** Allocated tips
d Employee's social security number 008-54-1482	**9** Advance EIC payment	**10** Dependent care benefits
e Employee's name (first, middle initial, last) Jamal Answar 257 8th Street APT 110 Atlanta, GA 30000	**11** Nonqualified plans	**12** Benefits included in box 1
	13 See instrs. for box 13	**14** Other

15 Statutory employee ☐	Deceased ☐	Pension plan ☐	Legal rep. ☐	Deferred compensation ☐

f Employee's address and ZIP code

16 State	Employer's state I.D. no.	**17** State wages, tips, etc.	**18** State income tax	**19** Locality name	**20** Local wages, tips, etc.	**21** Local income tax
GA		18,000.00	100.00			

1040A—PAGE 1

| Form **1040A** | Department of the Treasury–Internal Revenue Service **U.S. Individual Income Tax Return** | **1998** | IRS Use Only–Do not write or staple in this space. |

Label (See page 18.)

Use the IRS label.

Otherwise, please print or type.

OMB No. 1545-0085

L A B E L H E R E

Your first name and initial **Jamal** Last name **Answar** Your social security number **008 54 1482**

If a joint return, spouse's first name and initial **Radira** Last name **Answar** Spouse's social security number **008 07 8304**

Home address (number and street). If you have a P.O. box, see page 19. **257 8th Street** Apt. no. **110**

City, town or post office, state, and ZIP code. If you have a foreign address, see page 19. **Atlanta, GA 30000**

▲ **IMPORTANT!** ▲ You **must** enter your SSN(s) above.

Presidential Election Campaign Fund (See page 19.)
Do you want $3 to go to this fund? . . . . [Yes ☒ No]
If a joint return, does your spouse want $3 to go to this fund? [Yes ☒ No]

Note: *Checking "Yes" will not change your tax or reduce your refund.*

Filing status

Check only one box.

1 ☐ Single
2 ☒ Married filing joint return (even if only one had income)
3 ☐ Married filing separate return. Enter spouse's social security number above and full name here. ▶ _____
4 ☐ Head of household (with qualifying person). (See page 20.) If the qualifying person is a child but not your dependent, enter this child's name here. ▶ _____
5 ☐ Qualifying widow(er) with dependent child (year spouse died ▶ 19____). (See page 21.)

Exemptions

If more than seven dependents, see page 21.

6a ☒ **Yourself.** If your parent (or someone else) can claim you as a dependent on his or her tax return, **do not** check box 6a.

b ☒ **Spouse**

c **Dependents:**

(1) First name	Last name	(2) Dependent's social security number	(3) Dependent's relationship to you	(4) ✓ if qualified child for child tax credit (see page 22)
Jumur	Answar	008 71 3418	son	☒
Lale	Answar	008 33 2596	daughter	☒
				☐
				☐
				☐
				☐
				☐

No. of boxes checked on 6a and 6b **2**

No. of your children on 6c who:
• lived with you **2**
• did not live with you due to divorce or separation (see page 23) **0**

Dependents on 6c not entered above **0**

d Total number of exemptions claimed.

Add numbers entered on lines above **4**

Income

Attach Copy B of your Forms W-2 and 1099-R here.

If you did not get a W-2, see page 24.

Enclose, but do not staple, any payment.

7 Wages, salaries, tips, etc. Attach Form(s) W-2. **7** | 18,000 | 00

8a **Taxable** interest. Attach Schedule 1 if required. **8a** | 0 | 00
b **Tax-exempt** interest. DO NOT include on line 8a. 8b

9 Ordinary dividends. Attach Schedule 1 if required. **9** | 0 | 00

10a Total IRA distributions. 10a | 10b Taxable amount (see page 24). **10b** | 0 | 00

11a Total pensions and annuities. 11a | 11b Taxable amount (see page 25). **11b** | 0 | 00

12 Unemployment compensation. **12** | 0 | 00

13a Social security benefits. 13a | 13b Taxable amount (see page 27). **13b** | 0 | 00

14 Add lines 7 through 13b (far right column). This is your **total income.** ▶ **14** | 18,000 | 00

Adjusted gross income

15 IRA deduction (see page 28). 15 | 0 | 00

16 Student loan interest deduction (see page 28). 16 | 0 | 00

17 Add lines 15 and 16. These are your **total adjustments.** **17** | 0 | 00

18 Subtract line 17 from line 14. This is your **adjusted gross income.** If under $30,095 (under $10,030 if a child did not live with you), see the EIC instructions on page 36. ▶ **18** | 18,000 | 00

For Disclosure, Privacy Act, and Paperwork Reduction Act Notice, see page 49. Cat. No. 11327A **1998 Form 1040A**

1040A—PAGE 2

1998 Form 1040A page 2

Taxable income	**19**	Enter the amount from line 18.	19	18,000 00

20a Check if: ☐ **You** were 65 or older ☐ Blind
☐ **Spouse** was 65 or older ☐ Blind
Enter number of boxes checked ▶ 20a ☐

b If you are married filing separately and your spouse itemizes deductions, see page 30 and check here . . . . . . ▶ 20b ☐

21 Enter the **standard deduction** for your filing status. **But** see page 31 if you checked any box on line 20a or 20b **OR** if someone can claim you as a dependent.
- Single—$4,250 • Married filing jointly or Qualifying widow(er)—$7,100
- Head of household—$6,250 • Married filing separately—$3,550   **21** 7,100 00

22	Subtract line 21 from line 19. If line 21 is more than line 19, enter -0-. **22**	10,900 00
23	Multiply $2,700 by the total number of exemptions claimed on line 6d. **23**	10,800 00
24	Subtract line 23 from line 22. If line 23 is more than line 22, enter -0-. This is your **taxable income**. ▶ **24**	100 00

Tax, credits, and payments

25	Find the tax on the amount on line 24 (see page 31). **25**	17 00
26	Credit for child and dependent care expenses. Attach Schedule 2. **26** 0 00	
27	Credit for the elderly or the disabled. Attach Schedule 3. **27** 0 00	
28	Child tax credit (see page 32). **28** 17 00	
29	Education credits. Attach Form 8863. **29** 0 00	
30	Adoption credit. Attach Form 8839. **30** 0 00	
31	Add lines 26 through 30. These are your **total credits**. **31**	17 00
32	Subtract line 31 from line 25. If line 31 is more than line 25, enter -0-. **32**	0 00
33	Advance earned income credit payments from Form(s) W-2. **33**	0 00
34	Add lines 32 and 33. This is your **total tax**. ▶ **34**	0 00
35	Total Federal income tax withheld from Forms W-2 and 1099. **35** 400 00	
36	1998 estimated tax payments and amount applied from 1997 return. **36** 0 00	
37a	**Earned income credit.** Attach Schedule EIC if you have a qualifying child. **37a** EIC	
b	Nontaxable earned income: amount ▶ and type ▶	
38	Additional child tax credit. Attach Form 8812. **38**	
39	Add lines 35, 36, 37a, and 38. These are your **total payments**. ▶ **39**	

Refund

Have it directly deposited! See page 43 and fill in 41b, 41c, and 41d.

40	If line 39 is more than line 34, subtract line 34 from line 39. This is the amount you **overpaid**. **40**	
41a	Amount of line 40 you want **refunded to you**. **41a**	
b	Routing number	
c	Type: ☐ Checking ☐ Savings	
d	Account number	
42	Amount of line 40 you want **applied to your 1999 estimated tax**. **42**	

Amount you owe

43	If line 34 is more than line 39, subtract line 39 from line 34. This is the **amount you owe**. For details on how to pay, see page 44. **43**	
44	Estimated tax penalty (see page 44). **44**	

Sign here

Joint return? See page 19. Keep a copy for your records.

Under penalties of perjury, I declare that I have examined this return and accompanying schedules and statements, and to the best of my knowledge and belief, they are true, correct, and accurately list all amounts and sources of income I received during the tax year. Declaration of preparer (other than the taxpayer) is based on all information of which the preparer has any knowledge.

Your signature	Date	Your occupation factory worker	Daytime telephone number (optional)
Spouse's signature. If joint return, BOTH must sign.	Date	Spouse's occupation housewife	( )

Paid preparer's use only

Preparer's signature ▶	Date	Check if self-employed ☐	Preparer's social security no.
Firm's name (or yours if self-employed) and address ▶			EIN
			ZIP code

✸

1040A—CHILD TAX CREDIT WORKSHEET

Child Tax Credit Worksheet–Line 28

Do Not File

► Keep for your records.

1. $400.00 _____ **2** _____ . Multiply and enter the result . . . . **1.** __800|00__

    Enter number of qualifying children (see page 32)

2. Enter the amount from Form 1040A, line 19 . . . . . **2.** __18,000|00__

3. Is line 2 above more than $55,000?

    ☒ **No.** Skip lines 3 through 5, enter -0- on line 6, and go to line 7.

    ☐ **Yes.** Enter: $75,000 if single, head of household, or qualifying widow(er); $110,000 if married filing jointly; $55,000 if married filing separately . . . . . **3.** _____

4. Subtract line 3 from line 2. If zero or less, enter -0- here and on line 6, and go to line 7 . . . . **4.** _____

5. Divide line 4 by $1,000. If the result is not a whole number, round it up to the next higher whole number (for example, round 0.01 to 1) . . . . **5.** _____

6. Multiply $50 by the number on line 5 . . . . **6.** __0|00__

7. Subtract line 6 from line 1. If zero or less, **stop here; you cannot** take this credit . **7.** __800|00__

8. Enter the amount from Form 1040A, line 25 . . . . . **8.** __17|00__

9. Is line 1 above more than $800?

    ☒ **No.** Add the amounts from Form 1040A, lines 26, 27, and 29. Enter the total.

    ☐ **Yes.** Enter the amount from the worksheet on page 34.   **9.** __0|00__

10. Subtract line 9 above from line 8 . . . . **10.** __17|00__

11. Child tax credit. Enter the **smaller** of line 7 or line 10 here and on Form 1040A, line 28 ► **11.** __17|00__

TIP *If line 1 above is more than $800, you may be able to take the **Additional Child Tax Credit**. See page 32.*

EIC—PAGE 1

SCHEDULE EIC (Form 1040A or 1040) Department of the Treasury Internal Revenue Service (99)	Earned Income Credit (Qualifying Child Information) ▶ Attach to Form 1040A or 1040. ▶ See instructions on back.	OMB No. 1545-0074 **1998** Attachment Sequence No. **43**

Name(s) shown on return Jamal and Radira Answar

Your social security number 008 54 1482

Before you begin . . .

- See the instructions for Form 1040A, lines 37a and 37b, or Form 1040, lines 59a and 59b, to find out if you can take this credit.
- If you can take the credit, fill in the Earned Income Credit Worksheet in the Form 1040A or Form 1040 instructions to figure your credit. **But if you want the IRS to figure it for you, see instructions on back.**

Then, you **must** complete and attach Schedule EIC only if you have a qualifying child (see boxes on back).

Information About Your Qualifying Child or Children

If you have more than two qualifying children, you only have to list two to get the maximum credit.

Caution: *If you do not attach Schedule EIC and fill in all the lines that apply, it will take us longer to process your return and issue your refund.*	**Child 1**		**Child 2**	
1 Child's name	First name Jumur	Last name Answar	First name Lale	Last name Answar
2 Child's year of birth	19 9 6		19 9 7	
3 If the child was born **before 1980** AND—				
a was **under age 24** at the end of 1998 **and** a student, check "Yes," **OR**	☐ Yes		☐ Yes	
b was permanently and totally disabled (see back), check "Yes"	☐ Yes		☐ Yes	
4 Enter the child's social security number .	008 71 3418		008 32 2596	
5 Child's relationship to you (for example, son, grandchild, etc.)	son		daughter	
6 Number of months child lived with you in the United States in 1998	12 months		12 months	

TIP: Do you want the earned income credit added to your take-home pay in 1999? To see if you qualify, get **Form W-5** from your employer or by calling the IRS at 1-800-TAX-FORM (1-800-829-3676).

For Paperwork Reduction Act Notice, see Form 1040A or 1040 instructions. Cat. No. 13339M **Schedule EIC (Form 1040A or 1040) 1998**

EIC—PAGE 2

Instructions

Purpose of Schedule

If you can take the earned income credit and have a qualifying child, use Schedule EIC to give information about that child. To figure the amount of your credit, use the worksheet in the instructions for Form 1040A, lines 37a and 37b, or Form 1040, lines 59a and 59b.

If you want the IRS to figure the credit for you, enter "EIC" directly to the right of line 37a of Form 1040A or line 59a of Form 1040. Also, enter the amount and type of any nontaxable earned income in the spaces provided on Form 1040A, line 37b, or Form 1040, line 59b, and attach Schedule EIC to your return.

Line 1

Enter each qualifying child's name.

Line 3a

If your child was born **before 1980** but was under age 24 at the end of 1998 and a student, check "Yes."

Your child was a **student** if, during any 5 months of 1998, he or she—

• Was enrolled as a full-time student at a school, or

• Took a full-time, on-farm training course. The course had to be given by a school or a state, county, or local government agency.

A **school** includes technical, trade, and mechanical schools. It does not include on-the-job training courses, correspondence schools, or night schools.

Line 3b

If your child was born **before 1980** and was permanently and totally disabled during any part of 1998, check "Yes."

A person is **permanently and totally disabled** if **both** of the following apply.

1. He or she cannot engage in any substantial gainful activity because of a physical or mental condition.

2. A doctor determines the condition has lasted or can be expected to last continuously for at least a year or can lead to death.

Line 4

You must enter your child's social security number (SSN) on line 4 unless he or she was born and died in 1998. If you do not enter the correct SSN, at the time we process your return, we may reduce or disallow your credit. If your child was born and died in 1998 and did not have an SSN, enter "Died" on line 4 **and** attach a copy of the child's birth certificate.

If your child does not have an SSN, apply for one by filing **Form SS-5** with your local Social Security Administration office. It usually takes about 2 weeks to get a number. If your child will not have an SSN by April 15, 1999, you can get an automatic 4-month extension by filing **Form 4868** with the IRS by that date.

Line 6

Enter the number of months your child lived with you in your home in the United States during 1998. (If you were in the military on extended active duty outside the United States, your home is considered to be in the United States during that duty period.) Do not enter more than 12. Count temporary absences, such as for school, vacation, or medical care, as time lived in your home. If the child lived with you for more than half of 1998 but less than 7 months, enter "7" on line 6.

Exception. If your child, including a foster child, was born or died in 1998 and your home was the child's home for the entire time he or she was alive during 1998, enter "12" on line 6.

Qualifying Child

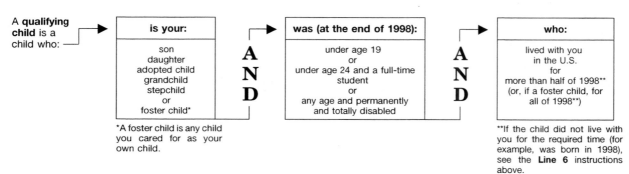

A **qualifying child** is a child who:

is your:	AND	was (at the end of 1998):	AND	who:
son daughter adopted child grandchild stepchild or foster child*		under age 19 or under age 24 and a full-time student or any age and permanently and totally disabled		lived with you in the U.S. for more than half of 1998** (or, if a foster child, for all of 1998**)

*A foster child is any child you cared for as your own child.

If the child did not live with you for the required time (for example, was born in 1998), see the **Line 6 instructions above.

If the child was married or is also a qualifying child of another person (other than your spouse if filing a joint return), special rules apply. For details, see the instructions for Form 1040A, lines 37a and 37b, or Form 1040, lines 59a and 59b. Also, the child must have an SSN (as defined in those instructions) unless he or she was born and died in 1998.

Glossary

Accountant—Person who prepares financial reports and gives financial advice. Many accountants prepare tax returns. An accountant with a special license from the state is called a CPA (certified public accountant).

Assistor—Person working for the IRS to help people with questions about their income tax forms.

Attorney—Lawyer. Some lawyers specialize in tax law.

Audit—A check of your tax return by the IRS. The IRS is looking for mistakes.

Claim—To list. For example, you list, or claim, deductions and exemptions on your income tax forms.

Deadline—Last date by which tax returns should be completed and mailed to the IRS.

Dependent—Person who is financially supported by someone else; usually a child. A person is considered your dependent by the IRS if five conditions are met. (See Chapter 4, "Who is a dependent?")

Dividends—Money you receive from stocks or investments. Dividends are a type of taxable income.

Earned income credit—A special credit for low-income parents who earned less than a certain amount. More than $3,000 may be received for this credit. However, certain conditions must be met. (See "Schedule EIC" in the Appendix.)

Earnings—Money you receive, usually from your employer.

Employer—The person or company that hires you to work.

Exemption—Amount of money you can subtract from your income for each dependent. You can also exempt yourself if you support yourself. Your spouse is also allowed an exemption.

Federal—Related to the government in Washington, D.C. Federal taxes are collected by the United States government. This tax money is then distributed throughout the country to pay for many different federal programs.

Fee—Charge or payment. Tax preparers who fill out your income tax forms usually charge you a fee for this service.

Filing status—How you define your family situation for tax purposes. You must select one of five choices: single, head of household, widow/widower with dependent child, married couple filing their income tax return together (jointly), married couple filing their income tax returns separately.

Gross pay—Total amount of pay you earn before your employer withholds federal and state taxes.

Head of household—Special filing status for single person who supports certain relatives. This filing status is often used by a single person with children. (See Chapter 4, "What is your filing status?")

Income—Money you receive, such as salary, tips, interest from the bank, and lottery winnings. There are many more types, such as alimony and money received from rentals.

Interest—Money a bank pays you for savings you have deposited there. You must report all interest on your tax return forms. (You *pay* interest to the bank if you have a loan.)

IRA—Individual retirement account. An IRA is a special savings account for workers, similar to a pension or retirement plan at work. You can deduct IRA contributions, up to a certain limit, from your income. IRAs represent another way to lower the taxes you must pay the government.

IRS—The Internal Revenue Service—the federal agency responsible for collecting tax moneys owed to the federal government.

ITIN—The Individual Taxpayer Identification number can be substituted for the Social Security number for tax purposes when taxpayers and their dependents are not eligible for a Social Security number. Use Form W-7 to apply for an ITI number.

Itemized deduction—The actual amount of expenditures you can subtract from your income. Use this amount only if it is larger than the standard deduction.

Net pay—Amount of pay you receive after your employer withholds federal and state taxes.

Penalty—A fine for not following IRS rules. Usually, the IRS charges you extra money if you send in your income tax forms late or if you do not pay all of the tax money that you owe. In very serious cases, such as fraud, penalties may include going to jail.

Sighted—Not blind. Only sighted people should complete the 1040EZ. Blind people should complete the 1040A form because an extra exemption is allowed by the government to blind taxpayers. This exemption is only listed on the 1040A and the 1040 forms, not on the 1040EZ.

Standard deduction—A fixed amount of money that the government allows you to subtract from the income you report to the IRS. The amount varies according to your filing status.

State—Related to the government of one of the individual 50 U.S. states. State taxes are collected by the states, then distributed throughout the state to pay for many different programs.

Support—Paying for such things as rent, food, clothes, medical and educational expenses for another person. Parents usually support their children.

Tax—Money collected by the state of the federal government to pay for programs they support.

Taxable income—Income upon which you must pay taxes. Not all income is taxed. Welfare benefits, workers' compensation benefits, and health insurance benefits are examples of untaxed income. However, wages, tips, interest from the bank, and lottery winnings are examples of taxable income.

Tax-exempt—Not taxable. Some types of interest and dividends are not taxable because they are received from municipal bonds or from special tax-exempt agencies like public utilities.

Tax return—Report you file every year to calculate your exact tax bill. Examples of tax return forms are the 1040EZ and 1040A.

W-2 form—The form your employer sends you in January each year showing how much you earned the year before and how much was deducted from your earnings to pay federal and state taxes.

W-4 form—Form completed by the employee that tells the employer the amount of money that should be deducted from the gross pay and sent to the federal and state governments as taxes.

Wages—Money you are paid by your employer; salary.

Widow/widower—Person whose spouse has died. *Widow* refers to a woman, *widower* to a man. There is a special filing status for individuals who lost their spouse less than two years ago, have not remarried, AND have at least one dependent child.

Withhold—To deduct money from your pay. Your employer withholds money from your paycheck to pay federal and state taxes. The amount your employer withholds is only an estimate of what you owe. The yearly tax return form is used to calculate your exact tax bill.